The German Ridi

BOOK 2

Advanced Techniques of Riding

The Official Handbook of The
German National Equestrian

3a

Kenilworth Press

© FN-Verlag der Deutschen Reiterlichen Vereinigung GmbH
approves this edition of 'Richtlinien für Reiten und Fahren,
Band II'

English language edition
© 1986 and 1992 The Kenilworth Press Ltd

The Kenilworth Press Ltd
Addington
Buckingham
MK18 2JR

Reprinted in enlarged edition 1992

Translation and illustrations by **Gisela Holstein**
Consultant **Jane Kidd**
Designer **Alan Hamp**

Phototypeset by York House Typographics, London
Printed in Great Britain by Hollen Street Press Ltd,
Slough, Berks

British Library Cataloguing-in-Publication Data
A catalogue record for this book is available from
the British Library

ISBN 1 872082 33 5

Contents

Contents

SECTION ONE
Dressage

1. History of the Art of Riding

We will begin by reviewing the history of the art of riding from its beginnings long before Christ up to today. It will help the rider to understand the ideology of training the horse and it will also help to keep the ages-old riding accomplishments alive and thriving.

1 (1) From Ancient Times to the Re-birth of the Art of Riding in the 16th Century

The teachings of the Greek Xenophon (4th Century BC) are the foundation of present knowledge and methods of training.

The guidelines laid down in his works *The Art of Riding* and *The Cavalry Major* are still of practical importance and are superior to the fragmented works of Kikkulis (14th Century BC) and Simon (4th Century BC).

Xenophon commended the same supple and independent seat as we do today. He knew the high school movements which were used to give the Athenian horseman a proud appearance during parades.

Xenophon also mentions in detail the cross-country riding which made parade horses equally useful for hunting and for warfare.

But there is something missing in Xenophon's lessons. The young Greek nobleman of the period rode only trained horses; the actual training and handling of young horses are not mentioned in Xenophon's writings.

We know from Greek art (the Parthenon frieze of Phidias) that the horses of Athens and Sparta were barely of medium height. They were bred in the Oriental-Thessalonian region, and since they had a lot of blood they needed very sympathetic handling.

Throughout his teachings, Xenophon's feeling for the horse's psychology is apparent. He could be called the first animal psychologist. This *feel*, although characteristic of Greek horsemen, was rare among the Romans, who imitated Greek horsemanship but could only copy the technical aspects without the creativity. In Rome, horsemanship reached no further than voltige and racing, which entertained the masses in the Circus Maximus.

Although saddles, stirrups and nailed-on horseshoes – already known to the Chinese before the Christian era – were used all over Europe during the 2nd to 10th Centuries, the art of riding hardly progressed during this period: on the contrary, during the stormy times of the mass migrations many established horse breeds were destroyed, together with inherited knowledge of horses. The art of riding was passed on merely as a caricature of Greek art. It was practised in carnivals and circuses in Alexandria and later in the eastern Roman Empire.

The knights of the Middle Ages also rode without any sophistication. Well-bred horses were used only as pack animals, to pull coaches, or for hunting with falcons. In battle and for tournaments heavy horses were used, their riders wedged into very deep-seated saddles with an extremely high pommel and cantle to prevent them from being too easily knocked to the ground. The horse had to thrust itself forward to give additional power to the knight's lance.

1 (2) From the Renaissance to Guérinière (from end of 15th Century to 18th Century)

Although the east Roman circus riders did very little for the development of classical riding, after the fall of Constantinople (1453) some of them fled to Italy, where they were patronised by well-to-do patricians. These refugees passed on their circus tricks, and revived interest in the art of riding. In the spirit of the Renaissance the classic principles which survived in the writings of

Xenophon were rediscovered and developed, along with contemporary saddles, and bits with lever action.

So the art of riding began to flourish again in Italian riding academies, with masters such as Grisone, Carraciolo and Pignatelli. During the 16th and 17th Centuries their teachings spread to France, Germany, Spain and England.

During the Renaissance the art of riding for practical purposes was rediscovered. The invention of firearms had eliminated the need for the heavy weight-carrier of the Middle Ages, and the lighter-footed Andalusian horse replaced the heavy battle horse, not only in man-to-man combat but also in games at court.

As already mentioned, one of the pathfinders in this rediscovery of the classic art of riding was Federico Grisone, who in 1532 founded a riding academy in Naples. Young noblemen from all over the Christian Occident attended this school. Similar establishments were founded in Rome, Florence, Bologna and Ferrara. Students were not only taught the refined art of high school riding, but also dancing, fencing and conversation, which at court had to be studded with Latin quotations. The horses at these academies had to serve as schoolmasters and therefore had to be schooled thoroughly to gain the necessary suppleness. The training methods involved were written down by various masters and scholars. In 1552 Grisone published *Gli Ordini di Cavalcare*. In 1588 the German Baron von Löhneysen published the first independent German riding treatise, *Die neu eröffnete Hof-, Kriegs- und Reitschul*. Although influenced by Grisone, the Baron rejected several forceful methods employed by the man from Naples.

Grisone's merit is that he adopted the teachings of Xenophon, following the Greek's criteria of a horse's carriage and a rider's seat but within the limit of contemporary saddles. Grisone emphasised trot work as a means of suppling the horse, which was unknown to Xenophon, who only used the trot for a few strides during a transition

11

to canter. Grisone also emphasised the necessity of securing the horse's neck at its base (in front of the shoulders).

However, in one important factor neither Grisone nor any of his compatriots (with the exeption of Pluvinel) followed the teachings of Xenophon; this was in the psychological harmony between horse and rider, which seems to have been forgotten and was often replaced by brutal methods.

At the turn of the 17th Century the forceful Italian training system shifted westwards to France, where its protagonists were two pupils of the Naples School: Salomon de la Broue (1553-1610), Riding Master at the court of Henri IV, and Antoine de Pluvinel (1601-1643), teacher of Louis XIII.

In de la Broue's writings the influence of the brutal Grisone can still be easily detected whereas Pluvinel's *Manège Royal* displays a timeless excellence. Like Xenophon, and like the horsemen of today, Pluvinel does not see the horse as an unwilling slave. He goes back to the horse's natural movements, which he tries to enhance, regulate and make more pronounced through training, without any loss of the animal's natural charm.

Among the auxiliary aids in use at that time were some two hundred different – often cruel – bits, as well as the 'gaule armée,' a long stick barbed at the end with a sharp spur. This was invented to replace the rider's sideways driving leg aid, the rider's leg being fully stretched forward, with the knee stiff. This standing seat was appropriate for contemporary saddles, and was similar to the position adopted by knights in the Middle Ages, whose armour prohibited any bending of the joints.

Apart from Pluvinel and his followers the riding masters of those times merely created artificial paces. The art of riding was deprived of its classic characteristics. It reduced the horse to a creature without will, misused and deprived of any initiative. Another sinister aspect of such brutal dressage was that young horses also suffered bodily harm. De la Broue confessed that many of his horses developed spavins.

Pluvinel, on the other hand, was known as the best French rider of his time. He taught the croupade, ballotade, capriole and courbette, the latter a 'half' or 'little' courbette, with the forelegs touching down after every jump (mezair). Pluvinel is also said to have invented the pillars. Whether they have been a blessing to horses or not is arguable, but at least today they are used only by experts in renowned establishments such as the Spanish Riding School in Vienna.

The Duke of Newcastle, who received his dukedom in 1665 and died in 1677, rejected the pillars, as he believed that too many horses were ruined by unskilled work between them. However, he still utilised part of Pluvinel's idea – with one pillar as a fixed focal point around which he worked the horse on a small circle. With the horse's head towards the centre he developed the suppling exercise known today as turn around the forehand in motion, or sideways volte. This exercise taught the horse once he had submitted to the one-sided inside aids to seek and accept the outside aids. This is the first step towards straightening the horse on curved and straight lines. It also prepares the horse for the collecting movement of shoulder-in, which is the foundation of all other lateral movements.

Gustav Steinbrecht, most famous riding master of the 19th Century, preferred Newcastle's *General System of Horsemanship* to all other writings of the 17th and 18th Centuries. Others thought that the Duke's methods were inconsistent and often unnecessarily cruel, although frequently on the right lines. There is no doubt that Newcastle had as fundamental an influence on his compatriots as did later the Frenchman François Robichon de la Guérinière (died 1751). Newcastle pointed out that for true collection the horse's hind legs have to be close together. He also knew how to use the snaffle bridle, the cavesson noseband and running reins.

What Newcastle did not realise was the importance of counter-canter and its advantages in straightening a horse and activating the hind legs, encouraging them to jump further beneath the centre of gravity. Nor did he use the well defined and exact aids of today's balanced seat, with its elastically bent knee and 'breathing', feeling legs. This discovery was left to the German Pinter von der Aue (died 1664) and to de la Guérinière seventy years later. Regrettably Pinter's early re-arrangement of the seat was little noticed, mostly because contemporary saddles forced the leg into an unnatural, stretched position, and Pinter had neither the means or the influence to redesign saddles. With de la Guérinière the situation changed, and he earned for himself an honourable position in the development of our art.

From 1730 to his death in 1751 he was Master of the Stables of King Louis XIV in Paris, and in 1733 he published the first edition of his classic book *Ecole de Cavalerie*. The fundamental knowledge and creative discoveries handed down in this book still form the basis of the training system of the Spanish Riding School in Vienna. A small flaw in the masterpiece is that although all movements are described clearly, there are almost no explanations of how to achieve them. In contrast to most of his compatriots, de la Guérinière taught, as we do today, that basic training is the same for every horse, no matter what he specialises in later on.

As Master of the King's stables, de la Guérinière was in a position to replace the then fashionable saddle (the *selle à piquer à la Pluvinel*) with the new flat *selle à la française*, which is still used today at Saumur. This saddle enabled the development of the modern seat, based on both seat bones and the crotch. The leg adopted today's position – no longer stretched but hanging down by the horse's sides, with a soft feel and ready to apply the aids instantly. It took half a century for this natural seat to become universally established.

Guérinière's main achievement must be that he

developed every aspect of the shoulder-in movement. With it he handed down to us the means of achieving 'légèreté', 'Durchlässigkeit' (the horse's immediate willingness to respond to the rider's aids), and obedience, without the slightest resistance. He recognised that the trot was the pace for all fundamental dressage work, although he did not appreciate the value of the counter movements, later explored by G. Steinbrecht (died 1885).

Regrettably Guérinière used the snaffle bridle only in the initial training period. He then changed to a Pelham with two sets of reins (double bit with jointed mouthpiece) or to a double bit with extremely long lower cheeks. He liked to use the cavesson with running reins, and made use of the circle to supple the horse.

Guérinière repeatedly emphasised perfect co-ordination of the aids as the necessary pre-condition for the performance of piaffe and passage and the high school movements above the ground.

To summarise, the most important achievements of this creative horseman must be that he wrote down the first logical and continuous riding instructions. They still provide the guidelines for today's dressage, in spite of some minor criticisms.

His tradition was kept alive in the 'School of Versailles', during the rococo epoch before being nearly lost during the French Revolution.

1 (3) Cross-Country Riding. Downfall of the Art in France during the French Revolution and Napoleonic Wars

Newcastle and Guérinière cultivated high school dressage more or less for its own sake. They neglected natural cross-country riding and military riding by cavalry.

During the 18th Century a new development took place in Prussia: *campagne* (cross-country) riding, was developed there and became an important addition to the art of riding on the Continent. But the development was slow and was not fully established until a century later, by Von Rosenberg in Germany and d'Aure in France.

Today we would call a campagne horse an eventer: a horse which is made 'durchlässig' through dressage training and which is also taught to like and enjoy outdoor work. The rider is thus enabled to arrive safely at his destination, riding across country over obstacles and water, taking the shortest route, and using up as little energy as possible.

The Prussian King Friedrich II and his generals (the most notable horseman being General Friedrich Wilhelm von Seydlitz) needed such campagne horses for their cavalry, and within a few years von Seydlitz produced cavalry divisions which were decisive factors in many of the great king's battles. This overwhelming effect of the Prussian cavalry depended on the training of the horses. The three qualities required were:

Speed, as the attacks were ridden at full gallop.

Obedience, to remain totally under the rider's control when in close formation. In face-to-face single combat they had to be agile and, in the words of the king, to be able to turn 'on a space the size of a plate'.

Safe across country, so that the cavalrymen could, if necessary, negotiate any obstacle in their path.

Campagne-riding utilising these three important factors was based on dressage training and developed alongside it.

Tragically, with the death of Generals Seydlitz and Ziethen, enthusiasm dwindled and the art of riding declined. The French Revolution and ensuing wars completed its destruction and encouraged the teaching of a more facile and hasty style of riding. Even when the Napoleonic wars ended in 1815 it seemed impossible to revive the art. French riders split into two groups, one following classic principles (though only superficially, for the sake of appearances and without meaning); the other practising a wild, purposeless cross-country riding. Both styles inhibited any worthwhile development.

East of the Rhine things looked brighter. The wars had not caused such devastation as in France. The Spanish Riding School still practised classical dressage, and produced teachers such as Seeger. In Germany Hünersdorf was the first German master of classical riding. At the turn of the century he was a 'Bereiter' for the Hessian household cavalry. Later he became 'Riding Master' to the King of Württemberg and was knighted.

He gave the art of riding new vitality and related it to practical riding, which was particularly important, as the devastation in France had caused a break-down between Guérinière's teachings and day-to-day riding. Hünersdorf changed this in Germany, teaching according to Guérinière's thoughts but never using dressage as a mere decorative art. Although he taught his pupils piaffe and levade on schooled horses, he never forgot the practical aspect of the art. Following in the footsteps of the Prussian cavalry generals he schooled mainly campagne horses, which after a two-year basic training had to be able to perform dressage, jumping and some cross-country.

In 1791 he published his book *Guidelines to the training of horses in the most natural and best manner*. This was the first classical German book on riding and training horses, and was praised by the French as the 'bible' for riders. It established today's balanced seat as the basis for the application of aids. The horse's self-carriage and relative elevation of the forehand were also defined.

1 (4) The New Masters up to Steinbrecht and l'Hotte

In Berlin in 1817 an organisation was formed 'to teach the training of horse and rider according to uniform principles'. This organisation was first based at the Cavalry School at Schwedt (Oder) and from 1867 at the Cavalry School in Hanover. From here the teaching of classical riding spread, and had a decisive influence on German riding.

One of the early teachers in Berlin and Schwedt was E. F. Seidler, who specialised in training misused horses (cavalry remounts in those days were mostly of wild, Polish stock). Seidler advocated unconstrained forward movement as the basis of an even contact on both reins, and relative elevation of the forehand. He also rode the horses across country twice weekly, and taught the rising trot, an innovation imported from England. He attacked the French circus performer Baucher for teaching his horses to trot and canter backwards.

The Prussian Louis Seeger (died 1865) also contributed to the development of the German riding system. He, too, denounced Baucher and called him the 'grave-digger of classical riding'. His motto was: 'Never forget that riding forward is the soul of the art of riding, and that the necessary impulsion must come from the hindquarters.' Seeger was trained at the Spanish Riding School and was the favourite pupil of the famous Max von Weyrother. In 1844 Seeger published the *System of the Art of Riding*.

In 1842 Karl Kegel published *The newest Theory of Riding according to logical and wise thinking*. In this book Kegel advocated the forward jumping seat, following the horse's head movement with yielding hands, and he explained logically why this seat eased the weight on a horse's back over a jump.

The same was taught by Count Szechenyi (died 1894) and by the 'official' inventor of the modern jumping seat, Federico Caprilli (died 1907).

Gustav Steinbrecht (1808-1885), a pupil of Seeger, was mainly interested in training horses for the circus, always according to classical principles. Many of his horses were admired in Renz, Carré and in American and British circuses. The famous lady circus rider Petzold was one of his pupils.

In 1885 he published his *Gymnasium of the Horse* which on the whole was a valuable guideline for classical riding, especially at a time when some riders had been led astray by the teaching of Fillis and Plinzner.

Steinbrecht's 'ride your horse forward and straighten him' became the motto for generations to come. He is considered to be the pathfinder of German riding instruction. The following is an excerpt from his book:

> The rider/trainer has achieved his aim and fully trained his horse when both forces of the hind quarters – the propulsive force and the carrying power – coupled with elasticity, are fully developed and when the trainer can use and balance the effect of these forces exactly.

The means of achieving this aim are rhythmic paces and 'Schwung' with a relaxed horse which is straight and moves in self-carriage 'through the poll', accepting the bit equally well on both sides. ('Schwung' is the transmission of the energetic impulse created by the hind legs in to the forward movement of the entire horse. An elastically swinging back is the necessary pre-condition.) When talking about lateral movements Steinbrecht repeatedly emphasised that straightness in the pure lateral bend gets lost (and with it 'Schwung' and regular paces) at the moment when the horse's hind legs no longer move on a narrow track (close together) towards the centre of gravity. Only when they do so can the horse's hind legs bend evenly, carry more weight and with each step swing straight under the horse.

After Steinbrecht there were a number of famous masters teaching at various schools of equitation (often army establishments) who maintained and developed the art of riding. There were friendly connections between neighbouring countries, and in order to gain experience army officers were exchanged between Hanover in Germany, Pinerolo and Tor di Quinto in Italy, the Bavarian Equitation Institute, the Spanish Riding School in Vienna, and Saumur in France.

During the 19th Century France produced General Alexis l'Hotte (1825-1904), who along with the German generals had an influence on the art of riding. L'Hotte was

Chief Instructor, and up to 1879 Commander, of the world-famous French Training Centre at Saumur. As well as being an elegant school-rider and brilliant all-round horseman he was a true psychologist, listening to the horse and always preparing it so that it could offer 'légèreté' ('Durchlässigkeit' with 'Schwung'). Further masters of the French School were Danloux, Decarpentry and Lesage.

1 (5) The Art of Riding in the 20th Century

Since the turn of the century we have seen some entirely new developments in riding. The most drastic changes have taken place in the world of racing and jumping, especially the latter, with the development of its new and extremely popular form – show jumping.

Racing, especially steeplechasing – which was a must for all army officers – changed in so far as American jockeys moved over from the fully stretched seat to develop the modern racing seat.

At the Italian army schools of Pinerolo and Tor di Quinto, cavalry officer Federico Caprilli worked on similar developments in jumping – practising and demonstrating the independent balanced forward seat. This seat had been invented decades earlier by the Bavarian Karl Kegel, but the world of riding was not yet ready for this development and few people took any notice of it.

After World War I, the show jumping section of the German Cavalry School at Hanover developed the new ideas in conjunction with established German training and dressage methods. This led to the German show jumping style which produced many international victories in the twenties and thirties.

During the first decades of this century the Cavalry School at Hanover was the leader and upholder of German riding knowledge. Many generals and high ranking officers helped to establish and maintain this position by winning international competitions.

In 1912 an army manual based on the theories of Gustav Steinbrecht (the HDV 12) was published. It still forms the basics of German riding instruction. In the same year the first Olympic Games of modern time; were held in Stockholm.

Because of World War I, Germany was not allowed to participate in the 1920 and 1924 Olympics, but in 1928 the Germans won the team gold medal and Freiherr von Langen the individual gold medal in dressage.

From then on the standard of international competition improved consistently. The tenets of the various countries became more uniform, and tempi changes became part of the dressage Grand Prix test. In Germany great attention was also paid to the standard of instruction among riding teachers.

All of these factors were to contribute to the unparalleled performance of German riders at the 1936 Olympic Games in Berlin 1936, when they won all the gold medals in the equestrian competitions.

The main purpose of the Cavalry School at Hanover was to train and produce instructors, thus spreading the German riding system uniformly over a vast area. The last surviving trainers schooled at the Hanover Cavalry School are Mr Habel, for eventing; Mr Brinkmann, for show jumping; and Mr Niemack, for dressage and training instructors.

At the end of World War II in 1945 the sport of riding in Germany appeared to have disintegrated, but, to the surprise of many people, equestrian activities quickly revived. Although there is no longer a cavalry to produce horses and maintain traditions, and although neither commerce nor agriculture has need of the horse, riding is becoming more and more popular as a sport and leisure activity. Today the equestrian industry is still showing a rising trend. A new type of horse is being bred: the ideal riding and sporting horse. The German National Federation (FN) is aware of its responsibilities in maintaining and developing German riding culture.

2. The Training of Horse and Rider in Advanced Dressage

2 (1) General

The German training method, with its systematic gymnastic and obedience training, provides the foundation for the usefulness of riding horses in all aspects of equitation. In addition to basic training it provides specialised advanced training methods for dressage, show jumping and eventing.

The German system is based mainly on the teaching of de la Guérinière (see Section I). He described dressage training as follows: 'The purpose of training a horse is, with gymnastic exercises, to make it calm, agile and obedient, so that its movement becomes enjoyable and comfortable for the rider. This applies to both the hunter and the school horse.' This statement of de la Guérinière still holds good today.

Based on the often used, but often misunderstood, words of Gustav Steinbrecht, 'Ride your horse forward and straighten it', advanced dressage training must proclaim the words: CALM, FORWARD and STRAIGHT.

Gymnastic dressage exercises as described in *The Principles of Riding* (Book 1 of *The Complete Riding and Driving System*) provide the basic training programme. The exercises and programme explained in *The Principles* are known as school movements. In order to advance, a trainer and/or rider has to understand that the horse should have already undergone a correct basic training programme, and that the rider must have acquired an independent, balanced seat so that he can give precise and correct aids. (The terms 'Durchlässigkeit' and 'Schwung', used throughout this book, are explained in detail in *The Principles*.)

2 (2) Advice to the Trainer

The German training and riding system has survived over many decades because it deals satisfactorily with all aspects of training the horse and rider for any riding discipline. But training methods are only as successful as the people who interpret them. The instructor and trainer of horse and rider must master the art of riding at his level in practice as well as in theory. He must be absolutely familiar with the aim and method of the training programme. He must know the purpose and build-up of, and the connection between, the various school movements, as well as recognising the difficulties and typical mistakes. Only the instructor who can himself perform the movements in the saddle will have the full trust and confidence of his pupils.

Basic training in a novice outline aims to make the horse supple and sensitive to the rider's aids. The horse moves in horizontal balance within its natural stride, the rider adapting to the horse's movement.

The aim of advanced training is to bring the horse into a state of maximum suppleness and obedience. By making the horse totally obedient to the rider's aids one achieves absolute 'Durchlässigkeit': the horse is most co-operative, can relax, bend and contract all muscles and joints to the utmost degree, and can therefore produce extreme propulsive power. In this state of total 'Durchlässigkeit' the horse can work in a high degree of collection up to old age without any damage to its health. This applies not only for advanced and high school dressage, but also for fast cross-country work and show jumping. During advanced dressage training, when the horse becomes gradually more 'durchlässig', the double bridle will be used more frequently because it allows the rider to give even finer and more precise aids. Much of the work, however, will be done in an ordinary snaffle bridle to make sure that no one-sided stiffness develops in the poll.

In training the rider, the most important point to

remember is that only a rider with a correct, relaxed, balanced seat is able to give effective aids. This is especially important for the difficult movements of advanced dressage. Only riders who themselves have been trained properly and who have years of experience in schooling novice horses should try to bring on horses to a higher level. Again, the principle *a novice rider on a trained horse* applies. A rider has to learn on a trained horse how to ride an advanced movement and to develop a feel for the movement. Only then can he – later on – transfer his knowledge to a less experienced horse.

Even a rider who has no ambitions of bringing on young horses to advanced level and is satisfied to ride or perform on made horses will still need the help of an expert to maintain his standards. Even the most experienced rider needs regular 'refresher courses'.

A proven method of improving the seat position is riding on the lunge, but regrettably too few advanced riders make use of this. On the lunge it is easy to correct any slight irregularities which might develop in a rider's position. The fact that the rider is being lunged gives him a good chance to concentrate on feeling the movement, and on the refinement of his aids.

Further advice to riders is to avoid becoming too one-track minded after having, for instance, specialised in dressage. Occasional riding across country, hunting, or jumping refreshes and establishes the necessary versatility.

Another point is that riders should try to ride a wide variety of horses. Every horse has different strong points and different faults and requires therefore different feel from the rider. In the end the horse is always the best teacher.

Faults which develop in horse and rider during advanced training are harder to detect than in basic training. Therefore the supervision of an experienced and alert trainer is very important at this level. If there are signs of a fault developing, less must be asked of the horse for a time to prevent the fault becoming established.

Only horses suitable for the job should be chosen for advanced training. Horses with conformation faults or a difficult temperament may require an unreasonably long and troublesome training period, often with unsatisfactory results. For training in advanced dressage there should be no time limit. Some horses learn faster than others. On average one can reckon on another two years after basic training to produce a horse to advanced medium level.

Even the most experienced trainer should now and again seek the assistance of another expert. At advanced level it is difficult to detect faults before it is too late, and a fresh eye can help to avoid wasting time.

There is no way in which it is possible to lay down a strict rule on how to teach advanced movements: it would lead to 'mechanisation' and the production of circus tricks.

More than 350 years ago Pluvinel gave us these great words of advice:

We shall take great care not to annoy the horse and spoil his friendly charm, for it is like the scent of a blossom – once lost it will never return.

2 (3) School Movements

In our training system various school movements are used to supple the horse further and to improve his versatility as a riding horse. These school movements are the lateral ones – shoulder-in, renvers, travers, and half-pass; flying changes and pirouettes.

Only after these movements have improved the horse's 'Durchlässigkeit', its proud unconstrained self-carriage in all paces, and only when the 'Schwung' has been developed and manifested in trot and canter, should one go ahead and start training high school movements. In dressage competitions, high school movements are piaffe and passage. Classical high school dressage also includes pesade/levade and the 'airs above the ground' (school jumps), courbette and capriole, which are only performed with specially suitable horses.

2 (3) i PRINCIPLES OF PERFECTING STRAIGHTNESS AND COLLECTION

In advanced dressage the horse needs a higher degree of collection. Perfect 'Durchlässigkeit' and with it effective collection, is only possible if the horse has first been straightened.

Ordinary straightness is considered in relation to the spine

'Relative' straightness. In dressage terms a horse is going straight if the inside hind leg follows the track of the inside foreleg

The horse's shoulders are narrower than his hips. The straight line of the spine as such is not sufficient and can not fulfil the requirements put upon 'straightness' in dressage. Our riding system requires a 'relative' straightness. This means that on all straight and curved lines the horse's inside hind leg follows in the exact track of the horse's inside foreleg. (The horse is able to do this because he has been prepared in basic training by the exercises 'riding in position' and 'shoulder-fore' (*The Principles of Riding*, Section 2, Chapter 2 (3)). The horse's outside hind leg is encouraged to move into the direction between the two forelegs. Then the horse is – in riding terms – considered to be straight, and the hind legs are encouraged to move 'narrow', close to each other. In true collection the propulsive power of the bent haunches can thus be directed into the poll and from there back into the haunches. True collection produces 'Schwung' and cadence in the paces, not just shorter strides. If both hind legs step further forward under the horse's centre of gravity, the quarters with bent haunches carry more weight and then propel the body powerfully forwards and upwards. Because the centre of gravity is shifted backwards and the quarters carry more weight, the forehand is

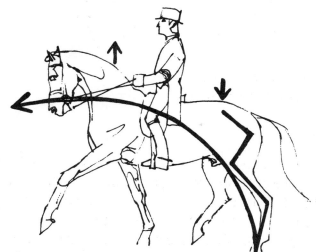

Collection

lightened and elevated, the horse's neck is arched – according to its conformation – and it shows proud and cadenced steps and strides. This is called 'relative elevation'.

Collection may never be achieved forcefully by rein action shortening the stride. Forced collection will not lower and bend the haunches, but the horse will step forward with stiff hind legs, and a tense back. The sequence of the paces suffers easily (flat, four-time canter, pacing walk). The most important rule for collection is: *The purity of the pace and Schwung may never suffer, but should be improved.*

Incorrect collection, forced by hand:
stiff back and haunches

Increased engagement of the quarters produces a greater 'Durchlässigkeit'. There must be an uninterrupted *FLOW* from behind forwards, and returning from the front backwards. Only when this flow is uninterrupted by any resistance from the horse will one achieve the springy, elastic co-ordination between the quarters and forehand which is necessary for true collection. Then we can improve the horse's paces and 'Schwung' as well as its alertness and responsiveness to the aids.

During advanced training the quarters will become more engaged and the haunches more bent and therefore more able to carry body weight and propel it forward. The muscles of back and quarters will develop and become more supple. The more this development progresses, the less the horse will seek support in the rider's hand. The horse will go in self-carriage with his neck and head held higher (according to his conformation) in relation to the lowered quarters.

There is no uniform position for head and neck suitable for all horses. The rider has to find the position most suited to each horse's conformation. The neck carriage is correct if – with the rider sitting correctly – the effect of the rein aids, supported by forward driving aids, flows uninterrupted through the horse's body into the quarters.

The ideal head and neck carriage in collection is when the neck rises freely from the withers, nicely arched, with the poll the highest point. The nose should be a little in front of the vertical, the bottom of the chin approximately

Dressage carriage

in line with the horse's hip bone. Such a head and neck carriage, 'dressage carriage', allows the rider a strong influence on the horse's quarters. It should, however, be asked for only during short periods, and alternated with periods of free forward riding in a longer, lower outline.

To check up on the horse's self-carriage and his ability to stay in balance in free forward movement, the exercise of 'giving and re-taking the reins' can be used. In this test exercise the rider's hands – giving up the contact – move forward about halfway along the horse's neck, touching the crest. Then the hands return to their normal position. This giving up of the contact is always supported by forward-driving aids. The horse's carriage and balance should not alter.

School movements which help to supple the horse and to improve and secure flexion, lateral bend, and straightness, are the lateral movements, starting with shoulder-fore and shoulder-in.

The most common and dangerous fault is to achieve the flexion in the poll and the lateral bend merely by pulling the inside rein. This makes it impossible for the horse to bring the inside hind leg forward and under. Simultaneously another fault occurs: the neck in front of the withers is overbent. This causes the horse to fall out over the outside shoulder, the quarters slip sideways, and the horse jack-knifes. The outside aids (leg and rein) should prevent the horse from falling out over the outside shoulder. The outside rein controls the bend of the neck and secures it at its base in front of the withers. In addition, the counter-canter is a useful straightening exercise, and suitable for this stage of training.

A further useful exercise to prepare the horse for a higher degree of collection and for lateral movements is decreasing and increasing the size of the circle. To decrease the diameter of a circle the rider shifts his weight more to the inside, and guides the horse with the inside rein supported by the outside leg so that he moves from the perimeter forwards and sideways – travers-like –

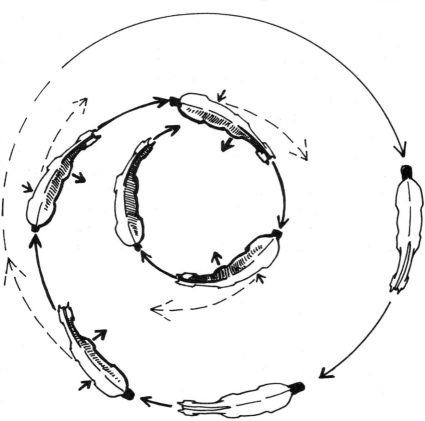

Decreasing the size of a circle

towards the centre of the circle. The forehand is always a little in advance of the quarters. The horse's bend will be more and more acute according to the decreasing diameter of the circle, and the collection will increase accordingly.

If the horse tries to avoid working and escapes by falling out over the shoulder and bringing the quarters in, the rider must use more outside rein and inside leg. After arriving on the small circle it is not advisable to stay on it for any length of time, and the rider should start to increase the diameter again straight away. This is done with outside rein and inside leg moving 'shoulder-in like'

31

on a spiral towards the perimeter of the original circle, which brings the horse better on to the outside rein. The rider must be careful not to push his inside hand over the withers towards the outside, as this distorts the balance and the horse will fall on to the outside shoulder.

Collection in the various paces can be defined as follows:

Collected walk In collected walk the steps are more cadenced and cover less ground than in medium walk, without any loss of elasticity or activity. The horse steps resolutely forward in a clear four-beat sequence on a steady contact. The hind feet touch the ground slightly behind the imprints of the forefeet. All joints of the

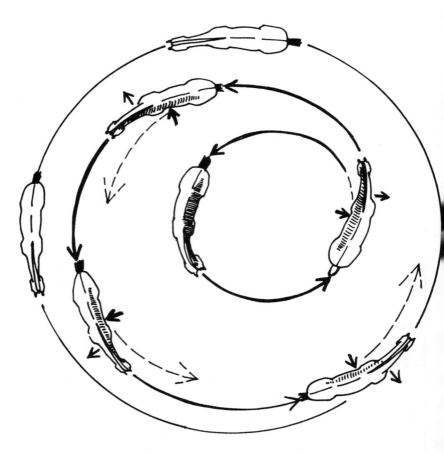

Increasing the size of a circle

quarters are more acutely bent. The quarters are lowered, and the forehand, with supple poll, is relatively elevated.

A faulty collected walk is one in which the well defined walk sequence is lost, so that the horse appears to be ambling or nearly ambling. Another fault is when the collected walk is slowed down only with increased rein action, the steps are slower and shorter, and the hooves are dragged listlessly over the ground. If these faults occur the rider must stop practising the collected walk and first improve collection in trot and canter. Occasional loss of rhythm can be counteracted by practising short sessions of lateral movements at a walk, followed by medium or

Collected walk

extended trot or canter to improve the horse's activity and desire to move forward.

Collected trot Cadenced strides in proud self-carriage are the characteristics. The bent haunches enable the quarters to carry more weight and propel the horse forwards and upwards. The transfer of weight to the quarters lightens the forehand and enables the horse to move the forelegs with ease and to stride lightly forwards.

Most common faults are a too prolonged moment of suspension, hind legs which drag, and loss of rhythm. Suspended strides are corrected by riding transitions into different variations within the pace and into different

Collected trot

paces. Loss of rhythm and running strides mostly occur in tight turns or small circles. The rider prevents this by improving collection with forward driving aids and by riding less tight turns for the time being.

Collected canter In collected canter the lowered quarters carry more weight. The horse canters in a proud, settled posture, so that he gives the impression of cantering up hill. The clear three-beat canter, the activity and 'Schwung' of the movement must be maintained.

The most common fault is the four-beat canter. In a clear three-beat canter the diagonal inside hindleg and outside foreleg touch the ground simultaneously, but in four-beat canter they are disunited and touch down one after another. Increased forward driving aids and transition to other variations within the pace can help to rectify this fault.

Another fault, caused by the horse's natural crooked-ness, is the canter on two tracks. Straightening the canter is achieved by cantering in shoulder-in position, and

Collected canter

increasing the forward driving and controlling aids. In order to maintain straightness in the canter, collected canter is ridden with a flexion inwards, even on straight lines. The rider strives to bring the horse's inside shoulder in front of the horse's inside hip, and with his outside leg he encourages the horse's outside hind leg to jump further underneath the body towards the centre of gravity with each stride.

2 (4) The Lateral Movements (shoulder-in, travers, renvers, half-pass)

The lateral movements supple the quarters, perfect the lateral bend, and increase the horse's willingness to obey

35

the leg and rein aids. They improve collection and shoulder freedom, and they stabilise the balance.

In lateral movements the propulsive power of the quarters is decreased, but the carrying power is increased without any loss of spring. Visible proof of having profited from the lateral work are improved paces and more ground cover in extended paces.

In lateral movements the horse is bent laterally and moves rhythmically forwards and sideways on two tracks. The degree of the sideways positioning of the horse's body depends on the degree of collection and lateral bend, and on the horse's conformation. Both hind legs pass one another closely, and step or stride into the direction of movement and centre of gravity. The lateral bend should be almost even from head to tail (the sacral vertebrae have

Almost even bend, secure at base of neck

Too much bend in neck: horse falls out over outside shoulder

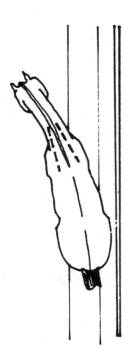
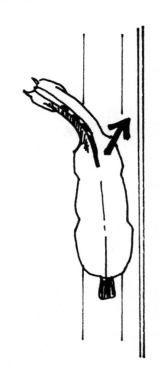

only limited movement, and for this reason there cannot be a totally even lateral bend from head to tail).

A grave mistake is too acute a bend at the base of the neck. It causes loss of rhythm and balance, and the horse falls out over the outside shoulder. The horse's neck must be secured at the base.

The more acute the angle of the horse's body to the track the more the horse should be collected and bent laterally. A hindleg should never be allowed to deviate sideways.

Lateral movements are mainly ridden in collected trot. Rhythm and 'Schwung' must be the same as when riding on one track. Riding lateral movements at a walk is used merely to familiarize horse and rider with the movement and with the aids concerned. Lateral movements at a canter require an especially high degree of collection.

Any lateral movement will have a negative influence, *unless* the horse, while still on one track, has first gained sufficient 'Durchlässigkeit', works 'through' the poll and is in self-carriage in walk and collected trot.

Lateral movements should not be practised for too long; at the beginning of training, a few steps or strides are sufficient. After the lateral movement the collected trot should be maintained for a while on one track to check that the purpose of the lateral movement (improvement of the collection) has been achieved. The medium and extended trot, which should follow, must show improved ground cover, 'Schwung' and energy.

In all lateral movements the rider must sit to the inside, with more weight on the inside seat bone. Pushing down the inside heel will ensure correct distribution of the rider's weight and prevent a collapsing of the inside hip, which would push the weight on to the outside seat bone. Wrong distribution of the rider's weight disturbs the horse's balance and rhythm. To avoid this serious fault and to be able to follow the horse's movement the rider must at all times keep his shoulders parallel to the horse's shoulders and his hips parallel to the horse's hips.

Collapsed hip, horse's head tilting

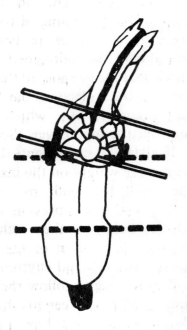

Rider's shoulders and hips parallel to horse's shoulders and hips

Another mistake which disturbs the horse's balance and rhythm is when the rider pushes his inside hand over the horse's withers towards the outside.

2 (4) i SHOULDER-IN

In shoulder-in the horse's forehand is brought about half a step inside the track of the outside hind leg, so that the outside shoulder is straight in front of the inside hind leg. The inside legs cross in front of the outside ones. The inside hind leg is brought well forward in the direction of the outside foreleg. The horse is flexed and slightly bent laterally away from the direction in which he is moving. The inside hock is engaged more and carries the most weight because of the diagonal position of the horse, the lateral bend, and the increased collection.

The object of the shoulder-in is to achieve a higher degree of collection as well as 'Durchlässigkeit', lightness and better balance. This, in turn, improves the horse's straightness.

The rider's inside leg, close to the girth, pushes the horse forwards and sideways, causes the lateral bend in the rib cage and engages the horse's inside hind leg. The rider's outside leg, a little further behind the girth, prevents the horse's outside hind leg from escaping sideways, so that the horse moves with both hind legs on a narrow track. The outside rein controls the collected tempo and the degree of bend in the neck, especially at the base of the neck. The inside rein merely guides the horse to the inside, giving the direction.

The rider starts the shoulder-in at the quarter marker after the first corner of a long side and rides without any loss of rhythm along the track. To complete the shoulder-in (no later than at the marker before the next corner) the rider maintains the rhythm while bringing the forehand back to the track and aligning it with the quarters.

In the beginning it is advisable for the rider to use the lateral bend of the corner and to start the shoulder-in immediately when coming out of the corner. Finishing

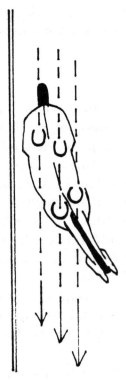

Shoulder-in

the shoulder-in with a volte is a good training exercise for the rider as well as for the horse. After the volte, either proceed straight ahead on one track, or again in shoulder-in, or alternatively in travers. Even at a later stage of training this exercise is always helpful to refresh the horse's lateral bend.

The most common fault in shoulder-in is the leaning on to or the falling out of the outside shoulder. This is mostly the result of too strong an inside rein action, causing too much bend in the neck. The fault is corrected by using less inside rein and stronger controlling influence of the outside rein with the hand carried lower and close to the withers. The rider's outside leg pushes and causes the horse's outside leg to step energetically forward. The rider has to take great care that the horse's neck is firmly secured at its base, in front of the shoulder, and that the outside hind leg does not step sideways.

When executing shoulder-in on the right rein, many

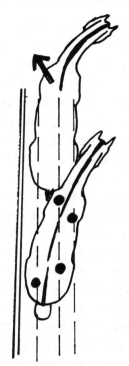

Most common fault in shoulder-in: overbent in neck, falling out over outside shoulder

Correct shoulder-in

horses are inclined to tilt their head, carrying the right ear a little lower than the left one. If this happens, the rider must ride the horse more actively forward, the rhythm must stay 'busy' and for a while the inside hand (right) may be carried a little higher but only for a short period until the fault is corrected.

Horses who come behind the bit in shoulder-in, although they are ridden forward, have to be brought back on to one track and ridden well forward from behind into both reins.

If in shoulder-in a horse shows slight unlevelness or loss of rhythm, the rider must first regain the horse's balance on one track by riding working trot and collected canter. Only when in balance again should he restart the work in shoulder-in, and then only for short sessions.

In advanced training, collection can be improved and the shoulder-in perfected by riding it also through the corners, on the short sides of the school and down the centre line without the support of the walls.

2 (4) ii TRAVERS

Travers is used to perfect and manifest the results of the shoulder-in: engagement of the quarters, collection as well as flexion and lateral bend. The benefit of working in travers is not the crossing over of the outside hind leg, but the increased engagement of the inside hind leg, which has to bend more and carry more weight. In addition it encourages a better overall obedience to leg and rein aids.

In travers the horse's quarters are brought into the school so that the outside hind leg moves a little inside the track of the inside foreleg in line behind the inside shoulder. The horse moves into the direction of flexion and bend. The outside legs cross over in front of the inside ones, with the hind legs moving close together towards the centre of gravity. The inside hind leg carries more weight and is more bent in all its joints because the horse's mass is moved sideways across it.

Before starting the travers the rider straightens the horse at the beginning of the long side. At the first marker the rider's outside leg pushes the horse's quarters into the school; he pushes in rhythm with the movement at the

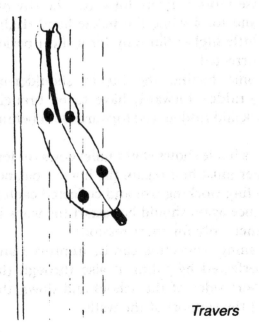

Travers

moment when the outside hind leg is leaving the ground. The horse's body will then be at such an angle that the outside hind leg moves inside the track of the inside foreleg.

The rider's inside leg close to the girth activates the horse's inside hind leg. Together with the inside rein it creates and maintains the correct lateral bend. The outside rein controls the degree of bend, secures the position of the neck at its base and supports the influence of the rider's outside leg. The rider's outside leg is placed in a sideways driving position further behind the girth. Together with the inside rein it maintains the sideways movement of the horse.

Lateral bend and collection are achieved by the rider's inside leg, but only if the horse is absolutely obedient to the outside aids.

To finish the travers correctly and to return to riding on one track, the horse's forehand is brought into the school and aligned with the quarters. Then, maintaining the

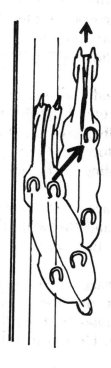

Finishing a travers: the forehand is aligned with the quarters

flexion in the poll, the otherwise straightened horse is brought with the inside leg aids sideways back to the track on the long side. This should be done in good time, so that when reaching the corner marker the horse is back on the track and totally straight.

Like other lateral movements the travers produces the best suppling effect in collected trot. In walk it merely teaches horse and rider to co-ordinate the aids. Performed in canter it increases collection.

A successive exercise of shoulder-in . . . volte . . . travers improves the horse's 'Durchlässigkeit' and lateral bend and his obedience to the aids, which have to be extremely well defined and well timed. The transitions have to be ridden fluently forward, with the horse's lateral bend remaining unaltered.

The most common fault in travers is to bend the horse's neck too much in front of the shoulders and to bring the quarters in too much, so that the slightly bent body of the horse forms too steep an angle to the track. Then the outside lateral pair of legs has to cross too far over the inside pair, the pace suffers, and the original purpose of the travers is not achieved. The horse's inside hind leg will escape sideways instead of carrying more weight and becoming more engaged.

Increased use of the inside leg aid and outside rein, which secures the horse's neck in front of the shoulders, will cure the fault and will minimally lessen the angle to the track so that the horse's outside hip follows just inside the horse's inside shoulder. Proceeding in shoulder-in is another helpful correction.

Should the horse show irregular paces or faulty carriage the rider must abandon the travers and energetically ride straight ahead, re-establishing the horse's basic obedience.

In travers the rider must avoid exaggerated transfer of weight. It should be transferred to the inside, but the active use of the outside leg often causes the rider to shift his weight to the outside seat bone. He will then be left

Faulty seat of rider in travers: inside hand pushed over the mane, collapsed inside hip

behind the movement and will tend to compensate by collapsing his inside hip and doing too much with the inside rein. In this position the inside hand is brought over the wither towards the outside – which is, of course, a fault.

When starting to teach a horse the travers, transition into travers is simplified if the rider utilises the lateral bend in the corner and starts the travers immediately out of the corner, at the moment when the shoulder reaches the point where the straight track of the long side starts.

2 (4) iii RENVERS

In renvers, as in shoulder-in, the horse's forehand moves on a track half a step inside the track of the inside hind foot. But, in contrast to shoulder-in, the horse is flexed and bent *towards* the direction in which he is moving.

The renvers is started after the first corner of a long side by changing the horse's flexion. The leg (now inside) and rein (now outside) bring the horse at the quarter marker in from the track, while the rider's outside leg keeps the horse's quarters on the track. To complete the renvers the

45

rider aligns the horse's forehand again with its quarters by driving forward with both legs and opening the inside rein. On the track the horse is straightened.

To teach a horse renvers the following exercise is suggested: shoulder-in . . . half-pirouette . . . renvers. The rider rides shoulder-in along the long side until the marker before the corner. There he executes a half-pirouette and, without having to change the horse's bend, follows the track down the long side again, this time in renvers.

The horse can only maintain his balance in renvers if the rider sits correctly – weight on the inside seat bone, outside shoulder sufficiently forward – so that the rider's shoulders are parallel to the horse's shoulders and his hips parallel with the horse's hips. The rider's inside leg should push only enough for the horse to take lively steps, with his inside hind leg towards the centre of gravity. The rider's outside leg supports the horse behind the girth, maintains the lateral bend, and takes care that the horse's outside hind leg does not step sideways, but crosses close

Renvers

46

to the inside hind leg in the direction of the inside foreleg and the centre of gravity.

Renvers can be ridden at a walk, trot and canter. In collected trot it produces the best suppling effect. Rhythm, activity and 'Schwung' must never suffer while renvers is being practised.

The main faults in renvers are loss of rhythm, loss of activity, and too much bend in the neck with too little bend in the horse's body. In such a position the horse would have to step sideways rather than forward-sideways. The fault is corrected by positioning the horse with less angle to the track, by activating the inside hind leg with energetic inside leg aids, and by increasing the importance of the outside rein in controlling the bend of the neck. Occasional tilting of the head – the ear on the inside carried lower than the other one – is corrected by the rider raising the inside hand momentarily and increasing the forward-driving aids. Another method is to interrupt the lateral movement and to ride the horse straight forward in a higher variation of the same pace.

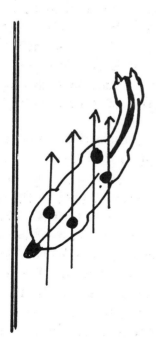

Most common fault in renvers: too much bend in neck, too much angle

Should the horse break into canter while performing the renvers the rider should not interrupt the lateral movement, but should bring the horse from cantering in renvers back to trotting in renvers.

In dressage tests, renvers is seldom asked for, but in training it is an excellent means of establishing the horse's lateral bend, as the quarters are supported by the wall of the school and the rider has a good chance to control the horse's outside shoulder.

2 (4) iv HALF-PASS

In half-pass the horse moves forwards and sideways along imaginary tracks. As in travers, the horse is bent around the rider's inside leg and is flexed into the direction in which he is going. The half-pass is ridden almost parallel to the track, the shoulders always a little in advance of the quarters. This is especially important, since the shoulders are slightly narrower than the quarters and therefore the inside shoulder has to be brought that little fraction more into the direction of the movement.

The purpose of the half-pass is the same as that of the travers: suppling the horse evenly on both sides and improving the collection by increased engagement of the inside hind leg. This effect becomes especially obvious in the counter-change of hand in the half-pass, through the change from one half-pass into the other. Half-pass is performed at collected trot or canter.

At first, half-pass is only performed for half of the diagonal (say from the centre line to the track or from the track to the centre line) or as a counter-change of hand returning from the centre line immediately to the track. In advanced training the half-pass is performed along the whole diagonal from one long side across the school to the other long side, or as a counter-change of hand along the centre line. The distance to be covered by sideways movement from the centre line is asked for in metres at trot and in a specified number of strides at canter. The counting is from the touchdown of the forelegs. To ride a counter-change of hand M-E and E-F the arena must be 60 metres long.

The aids for the half-pass are the same as for travers along the wall. Before starting the half-pass it is advisable to ride the first few strides in shoulder-fore position to make sure that the horse's inside shoulder is leading. The transition into half-pass will be especially fluent if the rider takes care that the horse makes the first step sideways with his inside foreleg.

When changing direction in a counter-change of hand in half-pass, the horse has first to be straightened after the first half-pass in one direction before he is flexed and bent into the new direction of the second half-pass. To achieve this straightening the rider prepares the horse with half-halts and with forward-driving aids, then brings the forehand in front of the new inside hip. This will, depending on the horse's obedience, take one to three strides in trot, or two in canter. The rider also uses these 'straightening strides' to introduce the new inside flexion

Half-pass

and bend. He does so with the new inside rein and new outside leg. At the same time he has to transfer his weight into the new direction by pushing down on the new inside leg into his heel.

The most common faults in the half-pass are a too sudden and incorrect change of direction; the horse tilting his head; loss of rhythm; and insufficient straightening. Changing direction from one half-pass to another often results in the forehand ceasing to advance sufficiently. If during training the rider detects signs of any of these faults he must stop the half-pass immediately and ride energetically forward, regardless of whether he has finished the movement or not. To correct any of these faults we advise riding on voltes, riding a figure of eight, decreasing and enlarging a circle, shoulder-in, renvers and travers, as well as transitions to medium and extended trot and canter.

The most common rider errors in the half-pass are incorrect weight distribution, collapsing the inside hip, which usually involves the inside hand crossing the withers to the outside. In counter change of hand during half-pass riders are often too eager to get into the new direction, do not sit quietly enough (especially when flying changes are involved) and cause the horse to throw himself into the new direction with the quarters leading. The horse uses these faults to escape collection, and to correct them the rider must reduce his demands. For his half-pass he must choose a line which has a less acute angle, and he must take his time when changing into the new direction. When practising half-pass with frequent changes of direction it is essential that the rider sits very still and concentrates when giving the aids and that he uses less new outside leg and thinks 'shoulder-fore' before starting the half-pass in the new direction.

2 (5) Flying Changes

A flying change happens during the moment of suspension between two canter strides. Most horses perform it running free in the field. Under the rider in dressage, however, flying changes should be started only when the horse is so advanced that at the mere hint of an aid he strikes off in a named canter anywhere in the arena. The horse must carry himself balanced and in a clear three-beat on both reins, as well as in counter-canter. The rider must be able to ride a very precise simple change with a given number of walking steps.

Only when a horse canters totally relaxed, straight and in balance, with 'Schwung' and sufficient collection, will he be able to do flying changes safely and regularly. The flying change has to be executed calmly, in rhythm, straight, and fluently forward. During the moment of suspension the former inside hind leg becomes the new outside hind leg which is the first one to touch down and to start the new canter stride. It is followed by the diagonal pair: the new outside foreleg and the new inside hindleg touch down, followed by the new inside foreleg.

The most common faults are an indecisive or irregular sequence of this footfall during the flying change: e.g. the diagonal touching down late behind or late in front; the horse's quarters swaying sideways; a slowing down of the canter pace, and the quarters being thrown up during the last phase, with the horse's weight coming too much on to the forehand.

2 (5) i THE SINGLE FLYING CHANGE

In preparation for a single flying change the rider uses half-halts to increase collection. During the canter stride, before the actual change the rider starts to give the aid by changing the horse's flexion into the direction of the new canter. The rider's new outside leg is placed a little further behind the girth to control the new outside hind leg, which will have to jump well under the body to carry the whole weight immediately after the moment of suspension. The new outside rein clearly supports the rider's outside leg in this function. The rider's new inside leg remains a moment longer in its old, supporting position behind the girth and helps the new outside rein to keep the horse straight. Only thereafter is this leg brought forward into its new forward driving position close to the girth, engaging the new inside hind leg. During the last phase of the flying change the rider eases the new inside rein slightly, without losing contact, to let the new inside foreleg stride out and touch down to conclude the third phase of the first stride in the new canter.

After the change the rider keeps the canter active and regular, with forward-driving leg and seat aids.

During the flying change the rider enhances the forward-driving aids by putting more weight on to the new inside seat bone. This, of course, has to be done without any visible movement of the upper body, twisting of the hips, or sideways leaning, which would disturb the horse's balance.

Most horses favour the change from right to left. This fact should be considered when starting the changes, as should the individual habits of each horse.

There are various ways of teaching a horse flying changes:

☐ Counter-canter on a 20-metre circle at one end of the school, and changing the canter when returning to the wall after X.

☐ Half a 10-metre circle followed by a diagonal back to the track. The last few strides on the diagonal back to the track are ridden as in travers and the change asked for just before touching the track.

☐ Changing rein M-E or M-K with flying change when returning to the track.

☐ Going large in counter-canter, the horse is asked to make a flying change in the corner at the end of the long side.

☐ True canter on the long side. Somewhere on the long side a flying change and counter-canter through the next corner.

The exercise mentioned last gives the rider an idea how well established the flying changes have become.

In the beginning it is especially important not to do too many changes at a time. One or two correct changes call for a break during which the horse is praised. It is practical to try the flying changes at the end of a workout, as this gives the rider sufficient time to prepare the horse and to reward him afterwards by ending the work.

The main problem in the beginning is that many horses tend to run off after the flying change – the cause being a sudden loss of balance in trying the change. In these cases the rider should first of all consider whether the horse was correctly prepared and balanced before the change and if he himself was sitting quietly enough and giving correct aids.

To calm the horse after the change the rider turns in canter on to a circle while giving and re-taking the reins.

If a horse finds it especially difficult to learn the flying change, in spite of being properly prepared, straight, supple and collected, then it is advisable to try the change at a more forward tempo while riding out.

Another method when working in an arena is to ask for a change over a pole on the ground. The pole is placed on the diagonal about 3 metres before reaching the track on the opposite side. While cantering over the pole the horse anticipates the new direction and usually offers the flying change. Repetition will in time teach the horse to obey the aids for the flying change without tension and to accept them even though the pole is not on the ground.

Some horses, after having learned the flying change, perform it correctly for a while, but then start making mistakes, such as changing late behind, not coming through properly, jumping a little to the side or swinging the quarters. The usual reason for this is the rider's position, and he should try to improve his seat and aids.

The following exercises will also help:
☐ While preparing for the change the horse is ridden

more strongly into the new outside rein, and the new inside leg gives a stronger aid.

☐ The rider sits absolutely still, prepares the horse correctly, and gives the aids accurately.

☐ The rider's new outside leg applies the aid more strongly.

☐ The rider asks for less collection and makes the change out of a more forward canter.

☐ After the change the rider continues in counter-canter to re-establish and improve the horse's straightness and collection.

2 (5) ii FLYING CHANGE SEQUENCES

In dressage competitions a flying change can be asked for every four, three or two strides, or 'tempi', meaning that the horse changes from stride to stride. The number of strides in a sequence should be counted at the touchdown of the inside foreleg.

Only when the single flying change can be performed calmly, straight, and at an exact spot, can work be started on sequence changes. To be able to perform flying change sequences correctly, a horse must have reached a high degree of 'Durchlässigkeit', obedience to the aids, and sensitivity. The rider gives identical aids for each change. The smaller the number of strides between the changes, the more the rider must concentrate to give accurate and nearly unnoticeable aids. The best place to start a sequence is along the track on the long side of the school, as the wall will help to keep the horse straight. The number of strides asked for between the changes depends on the horse's degree of training and sensitivity; eight to six should be sufficient. In the beginning the changes should always be asked for in the same place, later also across the diagonal when changing the rein. To start with, a little progress should satisfy.

When the horse makes a flying change every three strides, calmly, in balance and straight, the rider can proceed and ask for changes every two strides. Also, two good changes here are preferable to a row of irregular and unbalanced attempts.

It can happen that the horse when practising change sequences becomes too keen or misunderstands the aids and offers the changes too early or too frequently. It would be wrong to correct the horse harshly, but the rider should make a pause, ride different movements in a different pace and not repeat the sequences until a few days later. Depending on the horse's temperament, it might be advisable to go back to single flying changes or to sequences with more strides between the changes to build up the horse's confidence and to be sure that the horse will perform them correctly.

The main points to remember are:

☐ Before and during every flying change the horse should be straightened with the new outside rein.
☐ Before and during every change, think forwards.
☐ Before and during every change the rider's seat should stay quiet and deep in the saddle (invisible weight aids).

2 (5) iii FLYING CHANGES FROM STRIDE TO STRIDE – 'TEMPI' CHANGES

With every canter stride that the horse makes, he changes the lead. CALM – FORWARD – STRAIGHT should be the main characteristic of 'tempi' changes. Hardly any other school movement calls for such refined aids and rider 'feel'. Since the changes follow one another so quickly the aids must be extremely refined and a mere signal. If the rider jogs around, moves his legs too much, and changes the horse's flexion with too great exaggeration, he will disturb the horse's balance and the changes will jump from side to side.

When riding 'tempi' changes, both of the rider's legs have to stay in the position normal for the outside leg. They have to perform a forward-driving task as well as to engage the alternate outside hind leg and keep the quarters from escaping to alternate sides. Moving the leg noticeably forwards and backwards is wrong, as the aid would come too late and cause too much movement in the rider's position.

As in all flying changes the outside rein has to keep the horse straight, but under no circumstances should the reins block the movement. At each stride the outside rein restrains the horse while the inside rein allows the stride out. These alternate rein aids have to follow rhythmically with every stride. The rider should not lose the contact, nor must the contact become too strong. If the horse becomes too strong in the rider's hand, he will jump with the changes, which will be too flat and irregular, fall on to the forehand and come high with the croup.

When applying the very important weight aid the rider should not twist his hips and move his upper body from side to side. This would disturb the horse's balance and cause the quarters to sway from side to side.

With 'tempi' changes, as with all change sequences, there is always a great danger of mechanisation. The horses tend to get too used to the movement and perform it rather automatically, losing 'Schwung' and elasticity and coming more and more on to the forehand. They cannot gain enough ground, and seem to jump the changes 'into the ground'. To prevent this happening, or to correct it, the rider has to limit the number of changes and put a lot of variety into the programme. He has to sit absolutely correctly and to refine the co-ordination of his aids.

2 (6) Pirouettes

During a pirouette the horse's forehand performs a circle around his quarters. The radius of the circle equals the length of the horse; the centre of the circle is the horse's inside hind leg, which moves up and down with each stride nearly in the same spot.

Pirouettes are ridden in collected walk, collected canter, and piaffe.

A half-pirouette follows through 180°, and a full pirouette 360°.

The Walk Pirouette

The walk pirouette is described in *The Principles of Riding*. The ability to perform a perfect walk pirouette is the first step towards a canter pirouette. The horse is flexed and bent into the direction of the movement. The horse's forelegs and outside hind leg move around the inside hind leg which moves up and down in a clear regular four-beat walk sequence, touching down in the same spot or close in front of it. The aids are described in *The Principles*.

The Canter Pirouette

In the canter pirouette the hind quarters describe a very small circle. The clear well-defined three-beat canter sequence must be maintained.

The smaller the pirouette the more the inside hind leg becomes engaged and carries the weight. The other three legs, especially the outside hind leg, transfer weight on to it. The ability of the inside hind leg to bend more and carry more weight and propel it forwards and upwards is the sign of a good pirouette. The bent haunches enable the horse to remain in balance in the pirouette. Should the horse be allowed to come on to the forehand the rider would no longer be able to ride out of the pirouette at any given moment. The number of strides in a pirouette must be in proper relation to the balance and cadence of the pirouette. As many strides as are necessary are used to maintain the even canter rhythm. The number for a full pirouette varies from six to eight, for a half-pirouette from three to four strides.

As preparation for the canter pirouette the rider develops an especially collected and cadenced canter. The rider's active inside leg prevents the horse's quarters coming in as they do in travers, the preparatory movement for the pirouette. If the horse shows a tendency to bring his quarters in, the rider prevents it by approaching the pirouette in shoulder-fore position.

Without careful preparation the aids for the pirouette would come as a surprise to the horse, who would then throw his body into the turn with irregular strides. If horses show this tendency it is mostly to the left and it happens because in preparation the outside hind leg was not brought sufficiently underneath the horse's body. To correct this fault the rider must improve the horse's straightness.

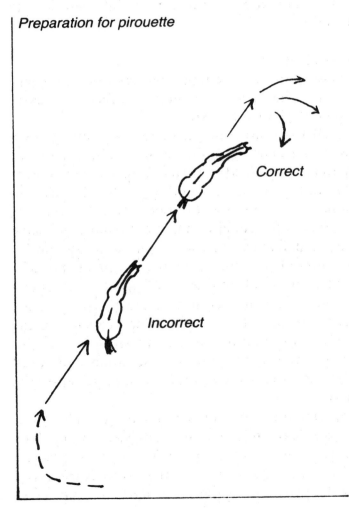

Preparation for pirouette

Correct

Incorrect

The aids are:

☐ The rider's outside leg further behind the girth, which prevents the outside hind leg from falling out sideways, bends the horse around the rider's inside leg, and maintains the sideways movement.

☐ The inside rein gives the horse the necessary flexion and indicates the sideways direction of the movement.

☐ The outside rein controls flexion and bend and helps to control the quarters on as small a circle as possible. It also dictates the rhythm. Under no circumstances should the reins block the flow of the movement: the contact must stay light and elastic.

Some riders have the habit of bringing their weight too much into the turn, which disturbs the horse's balance and rhythm. Leaning in too much and collapsing the inside hip has the same negative effect. The rider must sit absolutely still, his shoulders parallel with the horse's shoulders and his hips parallel with the horse's hips.

To finish the pirouette the rider guides the horse with outside rein and active inside leg forward on to a straight line. With increased forward-driving aids the rider re-establishes the 'Schwung' and activity of the canter, should they in some way have been lost during the pirouette. Type and intensity of aids in the pirouette vary with each horse and depend a lot on how high a degree of collection and straightness the horse achieved before the pirouette.

In teaching the pirouette one starts with the exercise 'decreasing a circle' in canter. But this time the horse moves more on two tracks, cantering in travers on an increasingly smaller circle. The rider should never force a horse round. If the rider feels that the horse is finding the small circle at the end of this exercise easy, he can start to train the correct pirouette.

At first the wall is used as a support. The rider canters in counter-canter along a straight line parallel with the track, about two horses' lengths inside the arena towards the short side. Before reaching the short side the rider

Short side

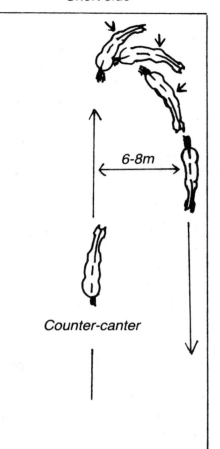

6-8m

An exercise in the
training of the
half-pirouette

Counter-canter

starts a half-pirouette towards the wall of the long side.
Facing the wall will help to keep the horse from trying to
move too much forward.

Little by little the turn can be made tighter. Even with
horses who seem to be physically well able to perform the
canter pirouette the rider has to use the pirouette sparingly. The horse's quarters have to work hard in this
movement and can suffer if asked to perform it too often.
For further training we therefore suggest the use of the
'working pirouette'. In this pirouette the hind legs move
on a small circle of 2-metre diameter, which is sufficient as

it involves the same aids and requirements of lateral bend and rhythm.

The main faults in riding a pirouette are escaping quarters, loss of lateral bend, loss of 'Schwung' and falling on to the inside shoulder.

The rider prevents or corrects these faults first through more careful preparation. Sufficient collection, and positioning the inside hind leg under the centre of gravity are most important. When the quarters are falling out the rider uses stronger outside leg and rein aids.

The task of the inside leg is mainly to maintain forward impulsion and lateral bend, together with the outside leg and the inside rein which is carried a little higher and flexes the horse at the poll.

If during the pirouette the horse falls on to the inside

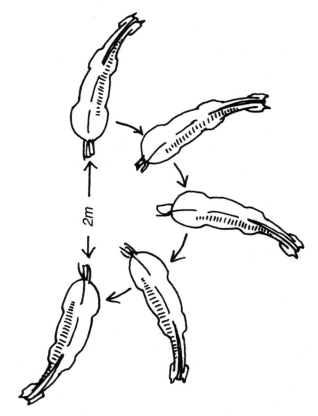

2m

Working pirouette

shoulder, the rider has to increase the 'Schwung' and straightness of the horse. To get the horse thinking forward again and under control he should ride out of the pirouette and forward on a straight line in medium or extended canter.

2 (7) The 'Schaukel' (See-Saw)

The 'Schaukel' is a prescribed sequence of backwards and forward steps without a halt in between. This exercise clearly demonstrates how well a horse is suppled and 'durchlässig', because only a very efficiently schooled animal can perform the movement correctly. The sequence starts from a square halt and ends with a transition into any given pace without an intermittent step or stride. After the initial square halt there is no further interruption of the flow of movement. After the first rein-back the horse steps forward immediately with the same hind leg that made the last step backwards, whereas the first step backwards is made simultaneously with the fore and hind leg which are most advanced in the last step forward. Within the whole sequence one should see a regular two-time backwards movement and a clear four-time forward movement. The 'Schaukel' is performed on a straight line with the hooves leaving the ground distinctly. The number of steps are counted by the number of times that the forelegs touch the ground: e.g. five steps backwards, three steps forward, three steps backwards, then proceed in collected trot without halting.

The aids are the same as for the rein-back ending in a halt. But in this movement the rider has to be even more alert than in the ordinary rein-back to maintain the forward tendency in the rein-back steps.

The most common faults in the 'Schaukel' are:
- [ ] Horse not standing square with his quarters well under him before the start of the movement.
- [ ] Rein-back with irregular, running or dragging steps and/or not straight.

☐ Loss of contact, coming on to the forehand and high behind.

☐ Pausing between backwards and forward steps.

All these faults are corrected by preparing the movement better, which involves improving the basics of the halt and the rein-back and making sure that the horse is really listening to the aids and is willing to co-operate.

2 (8) High School Movements

During the course of advanced training a horse might show physical and mental ability to progress to high school movements: piaffe, passage, pesade/levade and the 'airs above the ground' (school jumps), courbette and capriole. The piaffe is one of the most important high school movements asked for in today's Grand Prix dressage. The levade and pesade and the high school jumps are only rarely used (almost exclusively in the Spanish Riding School).

The high school movements not only perfect the horse's training, but even more they also perfect the trainer in the art of schooling horses.

High school movements give the rider invaluable experience and develop his abilities in all other fields of the sport of riding.

Since these movements are so specialised it is more important than at any other stage of schooling to be satisfied with very little. As soon as the rider can see the slightest progress he must stop and reward the horse. For the same reason work on these movements should take place only at the end of a session, so that after the slightest improvement the horse can be rewarded and taken back to the stable.

2 (8) i THE PIAFFE

The piaffe is a proud and rhythmic movement performed nearly on one spot. The movement is similar to the trot as it is carried out with alternate diagonals, but in contrast to the trot, in the piaffe there is no moment of suspension. Most of the horse's weight is carried by the well-bent hind legs, while the forelegs only support lightly. The back muscles work and the forehand is distinctly raised, with the poll being the highest point.

In the piaffe the horse lifts the forearm approximately up to the horizontal, then puts down the leg vertically, while the diagonal hind foot is lifted above the height of the hind fetlock on the ground. The horse's body moves up and down in a soft but very springy rhythm. On a trained horse the rider is able to control this rhythm with his aids.

A preliminary exercise for the piaffe is the 'collected trot in half-steps' (bending the haunches). As soon as the horse can carry himself in collected canter the rider can start to increase the bending of the haunches which will improve the carrying capacity of the quarters. But, again, do not increase the collection too quickly; do not work on it for too long a period of time; and never use force. After every success, the horse must be rewarded.

To prepare, or to perfect, the piaffe, it first must be

Piaffe

practised in hand without the rider's weight, and later on possibly between the pillars.

When the piaffe is practised under the rider the horse first is straightened and brought to a halt. From the halt he is ridden forward in 'half-steps'. With both legs the rider activates the horse's hind legs and brings the hind feet closer and closer to the centre of gravity. With half-halts and repeated easing and increasing rein tensions, all the time with a soft contact, the rider transfers weight from the forehand to the quarters.

The benefit of this work increases the more the horse lowers the quarters and the more energetically and actively he moves the diagonals. This collection 'in half-steps' should first be tried along the side of the school to prevent the quarters slewing sideways, and an assistant should help with a long, rather stiff whip. At the end the highly collected strides should be allowed out forward into a medium trot, or you should finish with a halt, making sure that the horse stands absolutely still and relaxed.

After a while the horse understands what is wanted of him, and his balance will improve. Then the rider can begin not to allow quite as much forward movement, so that the rhythmic diagonal steps cover less and less ground until the horse can do the piaffe nearly on the spot. A perfectly schooled horse will be able to do 15 steps of piaffe in rhythm and balance and only gain as much ground as the imprints of one to two hooves.

The aids to start the piaffe are similar to the ones applied to proceed into trot. The legs and the seat push the horse forward, but, depending on the horse's standard of training, the rider applies half-halts and allows each step out only for a centimetre at a time. The leg aids are given energetically but not tapping or kicking; the horse's willingness to go forward should rather be encouraged by careful use of spur or a slight touch with the whip behind the rider's leg; this will also keep the horse sensitive to the leg aids. Some riders are inclined to apply the leg aids in piaffe diagonally, but this can easily cause the horse to step sideways behind, or can cause the quarters to sway from side to side.

The main problem in piaffe is when the horse's legs are not lifted up as diagonal pairs. If the diagonal movement is broken, it is not a piaffe any more. Another problem is loss of rhythm, incorrect balance with insufficient lifting of the forelegs, often in connection with a high croup or upwards bouncing croup, and insufficiently bent haunches. A horse lacking balance will show this by balancing himself with each foreleg to the side, or by rocking the quarters from side to side. The horse's balance will also be disturbed if he leaves his front legs not vertically down but too far back underneath the body or too far forward in front of the body. If he brings his hind legs too far under, the hind hooves will 'stick' to the ground and the forehand will tend to rise as in the levade.

Most of the faults mentioned also cause the horse to drop his back, stiffen his neck and poll, and evade the bit.

Incorrect piaffe: croup high, haunches not bent, insufficient lifting of forelegs

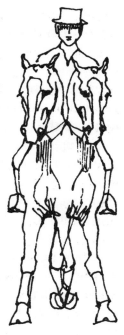

Incorrect piaffe: horse 'balancing' from side to side

Incorrect piaffe: hind legs too far underneath the horse, forehand rising

Every correction therefore has to start by bringing the horse correctly between hand and leg again, so that he listens to the aids. This is best done in medium or extended trot, in medium and extended canter, and in transitions. The trainer also has to consider the fact that different breeds of horses will perform the piaffe differently. Some breeds have a flat action, some a higher knee action. The latter will always show a more pronounced piaffe than the horse with a shallower action.

Only a rider with a well balanced, perfect seat will be able to ride a correct piaffe. The seat must be firmly in the saddle and the rider must sit absolutely still. The aids are applied with determination, but also with *'feel'* and must enhance the horse's balance and rhythm.

The most common rider errors are tension, stiffness, very obvious aids applied at the wrong moment, upper body moving, and hands unsteady and pulling backwards. To improve the rider's seat and feel it is advisable to teach him, without reins, on a horse doing piaffe in hand or between the pillars.

When horse and rider can do the piaffe perfectly they will be able to perform a pirouette in piaffe. This movement will show only very little flexion and lateral bend, otherwise the horse may lose his rhythm and the outside hind leg may fall out.

2 (8) ii PASSAGE

The passage is the perfection of the trot. It is a trot movement with an extended moment of suspension. The horse's quarters carry more weight and propel him forward. As each diagonal pair of legs is lifted it is suspended for a moment, enhancing the proud and rhythmic impression of this movement. As in the piaffe the horse lifts the forearm to the horizontal and the haunches are bent and propel the horse's body rhythmically forward, following the track of the forefeet. The more the horse comes off the ground, the more he lifts his legs, the more even the strides are, and the straighter the movement without the slightest sideways swaying of the body, the more perfect and beautiful is the passage. To produce such a beautiful passage all muscles in the horse's back contract and the loins are arched as in the piaffe. This does not mean that the horse should become tense. Although moving in the highest degree of collection he must convey the impression of being totally uncon-

Passage

strained. In passage the horse's 'Durchlässigkeit' and the rider's tact and feel must become obvious.

Before starting on passage the horse has to be totally straight and must have achieved a high degree of collection. He has to master the collected trot on the straight and in lateral movements and the rider must be able to make a transition from collected into medium and extended trot without effort.

Passage can be developed from collected trot, from 'collection in half-steps', from piaffe and from walk. It is up to the rider to study his horse and and then to choose the most suitable method. If the rider develops the passage from collected trot he has to prepare the horse with transitions to and from other variations within the pace. If 'Schwung' and 'Durchlässigkeit' are sufficient, the rider can start to increase the collection with half-halts. He then applies forward-driving seat and leg aids to bring the horse into passage. In the beginning he should only look for a few strides. The hands allow each stride out forward, and after the initial transition into passage the seat and weight aids are applied more mildly, otherwise the horse might be inclined to drop his back, stiffening the back and neck muscles.

When developing the passage from piaffe the rider uses increased forward-driving aids, which must not disturb the rhythm of the piaffe, and his hands allow the horse to move forward.

The number of strides in passage and the frequency of transitions into passage may be increased only very slowly: otherwise tension will develop, and with it loss of rhythm and straightness, leading to disobedience and thus a big set-back in the training programme.

When starting passage, as piaffe, an assistant on the ground can be of great help.

Under no circumstances should the rider accept the suspended strides if the horse 'offers' them with tense back, because this is extremely hard to correct once it has become established. The rider should correct this faulty movement by immediately making a transition to collected trot, a lateral movement, or medium or extended trot.

It is advisable to make the horse carry his head and neck a little deeper and rounder before going into passage, as the contraction of the back muscles is often followed by too high a neck carriage.

The most common rider errors are to miss the correct

Incorrect passage: suspended steps, tense back

moment to let the passage stride out forward, or not to be able to follow the movement sufficiently, or not to sit quietly and thus disturb the balance. The rider should be able to learn the aids and perfect his seat and 'feel' on a trained horse.

2 (9) Schooling the Horse without Rider

In *The Principles of Riding* it is explained how a horse should be lunged or worked in long reins. In advanced training, lungeing as well as working a horse in hand can be an additional training method. But always bear in mind that the work in hand can only be an additional help, whether with young horses when starting new movements, or in re-training spoiled horses. Training the horse under the rider is always the most effective means of schooling, and cannot be replaced.

2 (9) i FLEXING THE HORSE, AND ALLOWING HIM TO STRETCH

Although most problems lie in the horse's poll, some can be ascribed to the horse's jaw and cheek muscles – especially with young horses but sometimes also with older ones. The jaw and cheek muscles can be suppled in hand. This should be done along the wall, in order to have some control over the quarters. To flex the horse, the rider stands facing him. With his left hand he holds the right rein and with his right hand the left rein close to the bit. The ends of the reins lie across his left thumb. With the bit he applies vertical pressure on the bars, first softly, then alternately and evenly on both sides. This induces the horse to yield and relax the lower jaw. At first he will open his mouth a little, and then will submit and yield in the poll. The horse should answer the slight pressure on the bit by chewing or champing, but with the head not much deeper than his hip bone. The rider has to have a lot of feel in his hands, otherwise the horse could just open his mouth or come behind the vertical.

71

After the horse has reacted by champing the bit, you can start to flex the horse. He will yield in the poll laterally. To flex a horse to the right, for example, the rider's left hand applies pressure to bring the head slightly around to the right, the horse's right cheekbone coming closer to the neck. The rider's right hand simultaneously pulls the other side of the bit slightly forward. The left side of the horse's neck is very slightly stretched. The reins should not be used with even pressure all the time. The hand should be lively, varying the pressure slightly.

When there is the slightest submission of the horse the reins are yielded and the horse is allowed to stretch his

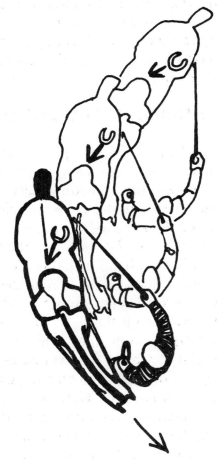

A first exercise in hand

neck. This lowering and stretching of the neck is the most important part of the exercise, as it dissolves any tension and stiffness in the parotid gland area.

It is important not to bend the neck at its base; just to flex the horse in the poll (causing the crest to 'jump' over from side to side).

This exercise can be very helpful in intervals between working sessions.

2 (9) (ii) COLLECTION IN HAND

Collection in hand helps the horse's training under the rider. It establishes understanding for the co-ordination of the forward-driving and restraining aids without the weight of the rider. The horse learns to go forward into the bit, to accept it, and to 'bounce back' from it to become light and collected.

If this work is done in short sessions with a fairly low degree of collection it can be started during basic training. With older horses it is especially helpful when they show resistance against the rider or if a horse has difficulties because of conformation. In such cases work in hand, involving less strain, can produce better results than prolonged work under saddle.

Work in hand also improves the horse's temperament: excitable and sensitive horses become quieter and easier to handle, whereas lazy horses become a little more lively and alert.

On the lunge the horse learns to listen to the trainer's voice and aids, and to move on a circle in side reins. As for lungeing, work in hand requires a quiet enclosure.

Equipment Snaffle bridle, a cavesson (optional), saddle and/or a lungeing roller, side reins, leg protectors (front and behind) and a lead rein or lunge.

The trainer needs a special work-in-hand whip, at least 1.50 metres long, springy and rather firm. For protection he needs strong footwear (*no spurs*) and gloves.

As mentioned before, this work should be done towards the end of the working session, which could have been ordinary flat work, jumping, lungeing or a ride out: whichever one, the horse should not be fresh or tense.

To begin with, the trainer makes the horse familiar with the whip, touching it gently along the back and haunches. Then the trainer leads the horse in to a volte and asks him with the whip to step forwards and sideways around the volte: first in walk, then in a quiet trot; first on the left rein, then on the right rein.

For collection work the horse is led to the side of the school. The trainer stands beside the horse's head, facing the croup; if he stands further towards the horse's tail end (e.g. by his shoulder), the horse's forehand will be pulled diagonally into the school. The trainer moves slowly backwards along the track, encouraging the horse to move forward with him. He uses voice, whip – touching the horse's hind leg above the hock – and the lead rein to move the horse forward. In these initial lessons the horse has to learn to trust the whip but also absolutely to respect its forward-driving aid. The trainer's hand should tend to stay in front of the horse. The horse's head and neck should not be too restricted.

Should the horse try to bolt at this stage of training, the

Collection work in hand

trainer should bring him on to a volte, then guide him back to the track again and make him stand absolutely still and relaxed before resuming the work.

After a few training sessions the horse should have learned to trust and respect the whip and should go willingly forward. Then the collection work can be started.

The horse should wear side reins of equal length, his nose one hand's width in front of the vertical and level in height with his hip joint.

The method of attaching the lead rein depends on the trainer's finesse and on the horse's temperament and sensitivity. The simplest and easiest way is to attach the lead rein to one snaffle ring or to the centre ring on the cavesson.

A variation is to have the horse led off the cavesson by an assistant. The trainer, alongside or behind the horse, uses the whip to move the horse forward in half-steps. Whichever method is used, the lead rein has to restrain the horse from dashing forward by using sufficient upwards-backwards influence. Together with the forward-driving aids this not-allowing-the-horse-much-forward-movement leads to the collection and bending of the haunches. The rein, supported by the side reins, is also used to keep the horse straight.

The trainer uses his voice and taps of varying strength of the whip as forward-driving aids. With the end of the whip he touches the horse immediately behind the girth, on the hind leg above the hock, on the lower hind leg, or across the back on the outside croup. The hand using the whip must have as much feel as the one holding the rein. The whip aid is applied in such a manner that the whole whip feels springy; its strength depends on the horse's temperament, but one should always try to use it as sparingly as possible. Aids which are applied constantly with the same strength make a horse insensitive, and should therefore be used only in the beginning and with extremely sensitive horses. Later on, especially with lazy horses, aids of varying strength are used. In the beginning the whip is used, together with the voice or clicking of the tongue, strongly enough to make the horse trot actively without covering much ground. Then you try to maintain the same pace with the voice and less whip. Most horses will keep up the rhythm, and only when the horse slackens pace is the whip used again a little more strongly. As soon as a response is noticeable the whip aid is eased off again. In this manner a horse is trained to collect actively on a gentle aid.

Only short sessions of this work are advisable. As soon as the horse works willingly and carries himself in balance with bent haunches the work is stopped and the horse praised.

When the horse has understood the basics of this type of work it should be executed equally on both reins. The ultimate aim is the piaffe in hand, with very little forward movement – approximately half the width of a hoof. Once the horse can do a balanced piaffe in hand the piaffe under the rider can be started. The trainer helps merely by supporting the rider's aids with the whip, if necessary; the aids then are gradually taken over by the rider.

Difficulties occur mainly if the in hand sessions are too long or if the demands made are too advanced. The horse then stiffens his back and haunches. The horse may try to bolt and refuse to collect. Warning signs are low forehand and high croup, loss of rhythm, and lying on the rein. Some horses try to creep backwards or to break away sideways. In such cases the trainer must first of all re-establish a clear rhythm, asking for much less, or even go back to lungeing.

If a horse lies on the bit and tries to avoid collection by coming on to the forehand and becoming high in the croup, it might be necessary for a short while to use a check rein, but the use of this rein has to be accompanied with stronger forward-driving aids.

If a horse lurches forward or is crooked he will lose his rhythm; this is most likely caused by the trainer's being in the wrong position. The trainer should be as far forward as possible, alongside the horse's head.

If a horse continuously tries to escape forward, use an assistant to stand in front of him and hold him with lunge and cavesson. Or, at a later stage, such a forward-thinking horse should now and again be asked to rein back for a few steps.

The main guideline for all collection work in hand must be the maintenance of a clear rhythm.

3. Further Training for Specialist Horses

Very few horses are suitable for even more advanced training, which includes work in the pillars, work in long reins, and high school movements above the ground, such as levade/pesade, courbette and capriole.

3 (1) Work in the Pillars

When the horse has worked satisfactorily in hand, and is collected, in rhythm, and relaxed, the pillars may be introduced for further perfection.

Movements suitable for work in the pillars are piaffe on the spot, levade/pesade and capriole.

Work in the pillars is extremely difficult and needs years of experience. It should only be carried out under supervision of an expert in this field. Incorrect or inexperienced training in the pillars can in a short time ruin a horse and even injure it severely.

Equipment Two pillars, a special strong leather head-collar, two strong lead reins, a lunge rein, two long whips, as for work in hand.

The horse should wear a snaffle bridle; saddle or roller; and leg protectors.

Two assistants are also needed.

The pillars consist of round timber or metal posts, 20cm in diameter, 2m high and 1.60m apart. It is essential that these pillars are secure in the ground and rock steady, to withstand the pressures put upon them. On the inside, each pillar has six very strong and well anchored rings, the lowest one 1.25m from the ground, the others above it at 10cm intervals. The whole upper part of the pillar must be well padded. The best place for pillars is at the centre of a circle, so that the horse between the pillars can face the short side.

The leather headcollar is of the same design as an ordinary headcollar, with no browband but with the noseband well padded, as in a cavesson. The horse cannot then get hurt and will be more willing to lean into it. The side rings must be strong and large, so that the lead reins can move freely. These leads should be 1.40m long and made from a double layer of strong leather. The hooks on both ends must be strong and quick to release.

The lead reins are of adjustable length, varying from 50cm to 1.30m total length. The lunge rein is 5 to 6m long and is held by an assistant while the horse is working in the pillars.

Pillar work is a specialized method for a very few selected horses and experienced trainers. In the wrong hands it would be cruel.

The expert will familiarize the horse with the pillars by showing them to him and leading him through them. Then the horse is worked for a few sessions between the pillars without being tied up. If the horse remains quiet and relaxed, the headcollar is put on and the horse is tied with the leads between the pillars. The lead reins have to be long enough to enable the horse to stand with his shoulders between the pillars; which of the six rings they are hooked into depends on the horse's height: it should be the one which is one hand's width above the point of the horse's shoulder.

An assistant stands in front of the horse holding the lead rein (or lunge) which is attached to the noseband of the headcollar. It is his task to keep the horse from dashing forward and if necessary to quieten him. The rider stands at a suitable distance behind and to one side of the horse, with a whip in each hand.

First the assistant will lead the horse with the lunge a few times forwards and backwards, to let him feel the limit set by being tied to the pillars. Only then can the trainer start his work from behind by touching the horse and asking him to move his quarters from side to side a few times. From this it is possible to appreciate why the horse will have to be well protected, with brushing boots on all four legs, and overreach boots, as well as having his shoes removed.

Only when all preparations have been carried out satisfactorily can the trainer carefully ask the horse forward to make a few piaffe steps.

Pillars are used for short sessions only, with a lot of rewarding and praise, and frequent variations to the programme.

The expert will have a feel for which type of work each horse is suited. If a horse does not offer a movement such as levade or capriole, it cannot be achieved with force. But if a horse does offer such a movement it can be slowly developed and perfected.

3 (2) Work in Long Reins

For work in long reins a well schooled horse who knows and trusts the rider is required. The horse must be able to perform all movements under the rider, and to be able to perform them in long reins on a mere hint of the rein and whip aids. Therefore the horse must be totally 'durchlässig' and able to trot and canter with 'Schwung', but covering very little ground, so that the rider can follow him closely at a walk, guiding the horse with the long reins.

The horse should be tacked up as for work in hand, but there should be no side reins. Two reins, each 4.50 to 6m long, are hooked into the snaffle rings. The trainer holds the reins at a suitable length. The loop at the end should be carried over the little finger of the left hand to avoid stepping into it. In the right hand the trainer carries a 1.30m-long whip, pointing it towards the horse.

First the trainer accustoms the horse to the feel of the long reins against his side, as when training a driving horse. When the horse is accustomed to this kind of work the trainer can control the horse with rein and whip aids while walking very close behind him. In this way he can work the horse through many movements, and can influence the rhythm, activity and lateral bend when in lateral movements. Experienced riders and horses can perform all lateral movements and flying change sequences down to 'tempi' changes and pirouettes.

3 (3) The Pesade/Levade

In the pesade the hind legs are extremely bent and are under the centre of gravity, carrying the *total* weight of horse and rider. The forehand is raised and the forelegs are folded at a sharp angle. The back forms an angle of 45° with the ground. The horse is in perfect balance, hence the name 'pesade' which means a 'weight'.

The levade is the preparation for the pesade. In the levade the horse does not raise his body quite as high and does not balance himself on his haunches for quite as long. Only horses who demonstrate an ability to carry out these movements in hand or in the pillars should be trained to perform them.

3 (4) The Courbette

The courbette is a sequence of several jumps. The horse jumps forwards and upwards, balancing on well bent haunches, the forelegs well folded with the knees high. He lands on bent haunches and jumps again several times in quick succession, without touching down with the forehand. Only after the last jump does the forehand touch down again.

Very few horses are born to do this movement and offer to do it. It would be useless and a waste of time to train any other horse to perform it.

3 (5) The Capriole

The capriole is the most difficult of all high school jumps. The horse jumps up, with the forehand and quarters equally high. The forelegs are well folded and both hind legs kick out vigorously at the height of the jump.

All these high school jumps are very rarely executed and only by especially suitable horses. It is therefore unnecessary to provide further explanations.

SECTION TWO
Show Jumping

1. Introduction

Riding a horse over fences has been part of the training of horse and rider since the art of riding began to develop.

In the 4th Century BC Xenophon provided instructions on how to jump ditches, banks and hedges. There are historic documents on hunting dating back to the Middle Ages which explain how riders negotiated natural obstacles. During wars in the 18th and 19th Centuries cavalry charges would not have been possible if horses and riders had not been schooled in jumping across country. In the 20th Century, though expanding population and industrialisation has reduced the amount of space in which riding is possible, the general increase in sporting activities has resulted in the growing popularity of show jumping.

Through the officers of the Hanover cavalry school the Italian school of jumping was developed and incorporated into the German training system. Results achieved in modern show jumping have proved that it is possible to train horses and riders successfully on the basis of and in co-ordination with established German training principles.

The horse required for this sport is 'losgelassen', moves in balance, obeys instantly in any situation and can produce enough jumping ability, speed and agility to satisfy the high demands of today. (The German term 'Losgelassenheit' can be interpreted as suppleness combined with looseness and with a complete absence of any tension – i.e. the horse is unconstrained.)

If the basic training of the horse has been carried out correctly according to *The Principles of Riding*, he should advance according to the advice given in this Book 2 and should come fairly close to being an ideal show jumper.

2. Guidelines for the Trainer

The trainer of an advanced horse and rider must have practical competition experience in these classes, because he will then know exactly what his pupil will have to face and he will also be able to assess if a horse or rider has a chance of success.

The rider should not be too tall or too heavy. He must be supple and have the necessary strength. He should have started jumping when quite young and should basically be an accomplished and well trained rider. He should have good nerves, powers of concentration, courage, and willingness to be self-critical. And he must have a lot of *feel*. Every horse is different, so to have lasting success he must be able to ride a variety of horses equally well.

Every trainer knows that it is a long road to success at top level, and few of the horses who show promise at novice level reach the top. Training a horse for top-class show jumping is not only a question of know-how and time, but also of money, therefore it is essential to be critical about the horse that one chooses. Only a robust and very sound horse with good nerves will stand the strain of top-class competition. Horses with faulty temperament are rarely worth the trouble, though sometimes a horse is only frightened because of unskilled handling or riding. It is difficult to differentiate this from a bad temperament and you have to get to know a horse first before making a decision.

As well as temperament the horse's conformation is a decisive factor. Feet, legs, neck and back are the most important parts. The most superb ability is worthless if the horse's legs are unsound. The neck is the horse's balancing rod; a short, heavy neck or one which comes too deep out of the shoulder cannot fulfil this function. The back co-ordinates and regulates the power. It must be elastic enough to conform with the curvature of the jump, the 'bascule', which not only involves an arching of the spine but also necessitates a stretching and swinging of the back muscles. A shortish, well-muscled back is preferable to a long one, which is often weak and over-sensitive to the rider's weight.

One important aspect of choosing a horse suitable for show jumping is something difficult to recognise: it could be called 'the will to co-operate'.

The horse should have a good technique, it should bascule, and should use the back well. The legs should fold well at all joints. The horse should not pull but be easy to ride, and careful.

If a horse is careful after hitting a fence hard he will correct himself and overjump the fence the next time. A coward will stop when approaching the fence again, and such a horse needs careful reschooling.

It is also advisable to try out a new horse over natural fences and over water. An initial stop is not too serious, as the horse might not be used to such fences or may be a little spoilt. But after showing the horse the fence and approaching it correctly the horse should jump it. Horses who do not respect water and keep faulting at it are more difficult to train than careful water jumpers.

Blood horses are mostly intelligent and can gallop but need a good rider and skilled handling. Stallions and geldings are in general easier to train and less complicated than mares. If a horse suits a rider and has sufficient jumping ability a few conformation faults are of minor importance.

Two more factors for the trainer to consider are correct equipment, and safety measures.
- ☐ A special show jumping saddle is essential. A multi-purpose saddle is not sufficient at this level.
- ☐ The stirrups have to be big and heavy so that the foot

can slip out unhampered in case of an accident.

☐ Bandages, brushing boots and overreach boots should always be used to protect the horse from injury.

☐ In national classes bridle and bits are confined to national rules, in international classes there are no rules concerning these items. An ordinary snaffle bridle is the most suitable tack, apart from some isolated cases. Severe bits lead to use of even more severe bits. The tack should not be allowed to camouflage the rider's shortcomings.

Avoiding accidents is always a priority.

☐ Correct riding gear, including a crash helmet, is essential, even in training.

☐ Suitable fence material in good repair reduces the risk of accidents. It should be properly maintained and set up, and should be cleared away if not in use.

☐ The going and its proper maintenance is a safety factor.

☐ Fences must be built to suit the rider's standard, never to overface or frighten a rider.

☐ Sound psychological preparation of the rider, and adapting the standard of training to his ability will prevent accidents.

2 (1) Training the Rider for Higher Grades – Improving the Seat

Success in higher grades depends on a sound foundation in the lower grades.

A rider will not make the top in show jumping if he does not have a secure dressage seat and sound basic riding knowledge. He has to master the basic jumping seat to be able to develop his individual style for top class jumping.

Between fences the seat depends on the rider's physique, the type of horse, the type of competition and the degree of difficulty. There are, however, two basic requirements which have to be fulfilled at all times:

☐ A supple body, especially in hips and shoulders, to be

able to follow the horse's movement quickly.

☐ A quiet seat: any unnecessary movement unbalances and upsets the horse.

The show jumping seat is secured by a firm knee and lower leg position. The lower leg must stay in contact with the horse's body at all times, and the heel must move downwards with every canter stride. The stirrups must be shortened, otherwise this leg position is not possible and knees and ankles cannot bend sufficiently. The tendency of many riders to ride too long makes their seat unsteady, while their upper body and lower leg move constantly and unbalance the horse.

The rider has to learn to change very quickly from one seat position to another. One minute he has to support himself on his thighs, taking the weight out of the saddle. The next minute he has to sit in the saddle and move his upper body backwards so that he can use the forward-driving aids to bring the horse together. The 'light' seat is a light-sitting seat, somewhere between the forward jumping seat and the dressage seat. It is used between

Light seat for jumping dressage and between fences

fences – often on the approach to a fence – and with short stirrups when working a jumping horse on the flat.

Suppleness in the shoulders enables the rider to carry his hands deep and close to the withers while maintaining a soft and steady contact with the horse's mouth. The hands are carried so high that when viewed from the side they are on a straight line between elbow and horse's mouth. The hands are also carried free from – not leaning against – the horse's neck. The fingers are closed on the reins, as an open hand, especially over a fence, allows the reins to slip through, which makes them uneven for the rest of the course. Stiff shoulders lead to a fixed and 'blocking' hand, which is the most severe fault in a show jumping rider.

The rider must at all times be in control of the horse. His forward-driving aids are applied with that part of the lower leg which is in contact with the horse's body, and if necessary with the seat by contracting the seat muscles in the saddle.

Over the fence the rider supports himself on his thighs and stirrups, with his seat close to but not in the saddle. Standing up too high is a fault, as it makes the seat insecure and any exaggerated movement disturbs the horse's balance. It is equally disturbing if the rider goes too much with the movement, bending his upper body down too deep and too far forward. It is sufficient if over the fence the rider's chest comes close to the withers.

After landing, the rider has to regain control as quickly as possible so as to be able to approach the next fence correctly. At the end of the landing phase the rider's upper body comes back a little and his seat comes a little closer to the saddle. To land softly and to sit into the saddle afterwards, it is essential for the rider's heel to be deep, acting as a shock absorber. This is only possible if the ball of the foot or the area just behind it rests on the stirrup. If the foot is pushed 'home' in the stirrup the movement is restricted and there is always the danger of a torn tendon in the rider's heel.

If the rider pulls up the heel the knee has to take the full weight when landing. This tips the upper body forward and brings excess weight on to the horse's forehand. In this position the horse cannot canter on fluently and in balance. A lesser fault is when the rider pushes his lower leg forward on landing.

A serious – and probably the most common – fault is the rider's tendency to carry his hands too high. A high hand hollows the horse's back, shortens his neck, and interferes with the bascule.

Apart from a secure seat the show jumping rider has to have the feel for a stride and for speed. The 'eye for a stride' and the 'feel for the pace' are achieved through practice and training. By jumping a lot the rider develops an eye for a stride which will enable him to adjust the length of it well before the fence, to arrive each time at the correct take-off point. The ability to lengthen and shorten the horse's canter stride enables the rider to make the related distance between fences fit the length of his horse's stride. His and the horse's eyes must therefore always look forward towards the next fence.

This is also one of the reasons why the rider should work continuously on his dressage. With correct application of the aids he should be able to make fluent transitions from working to medium and extended canter, and vice versa. The rider will then be able to ride a given number of canter strides between fences without altering the horse's rhythm and balance. Flying changes are also part of the training programme.

Gymnastic jumping is a good method of schooling the rider without placing too much strain on the horse, but it is common knowledge that show jumping can only be learned by show jumping. The aim is to produce a competitor: therefore it is necessary for training often to include riding a full course, and competing. This cannot be replaced by gymnastic jumping or by regularly jumping single fences and combinations.

2 (2) Conditions for Advanced Training of the Horse

To withstand the strain of advanced jumping competitions the horse has to be fully grown, five to six years old. The horse needs to have a sound basic training (dressage), must go straight in all paces, and must be equally easy to turn to the left and right. He must be able to make tight turns at a fast speed and in complete balance. The horse should halt obediently without any resistance in the mouth, poll or back, and should rein back willingly. He must accept the bit and must be able to canter on a named leg and make a flying change when changing direction. This flying change must be carried out in one phase; if late behind, it interferes with the rhythm, and loses time.

As well as all this the horse must have enough jumping ability. This is sometimes hard to detect, even if the horse has jumped successfully at lower levels. To find out, it may be necessary to test the horse over some bigger but fairly built fences.

Before taking a new horse into training he should be thoroughly examined by a veterinary surgeon, especially the legs, heart, lungs and eyes.

2 (3) Equipment

Basic equipment includes bridle, jumping saddle and leg protection. The best bit is the ordinary snaffle, together with a drop or flash noseband. In very few special cases other bits can be an advantage, but a rider should never resort to a more severe bit only because he is not satisfied with his horse's 'Durchlässigkeit'. This is a training problem and has to be solved by improving the suppleness of horse and rider. A more severe bit can only show an improvement for a short time, and then an even more harsh one has to be used.

The jumping saddle must fit the rider. Riders with long legs need a saddle with longer flaps. The particular build of special jumping saddles makes it easy for a rider to sit in the forward seat with short stirrups. There should be no need for pads behind the rider's knee, which limit the freedom of leg movement.

A wide variety of protection is available for the horse. Boots must fit the animal and protect his legs all round, and overreach boots should also be worn.

The most common auxiliary aid is the running martingale. When it is adjusted correctly the rein still runs from the horse's mouth to the rider's elbow in an unbroken straight line – but if the horse tries to resist upwards the martingale will give the rider additional control in preventing this.

The rider should not use any other auxiliary reins, either in competition or at home. The running rein can bring problems by enabling even a weak rider to put a horse into a 'forced' position. In special cases, however, the running rein can help to improve a spoilt horse, if used by an expert and only over a short period of time. If used correctly it should soon become unnecessary. It should never become a permanent feature.

2 (4) Basics of Course Building in Higher Grades

The construction and colour of a fence, its location, distance from other fences, condition, and the gradient of going, all influence the quality of jumping and the willingness of the horse. Riders and trainers are therefore well advised to pay great attention to every detail of course building. Fences used at home during training have to be as well built as at shows.

When training a horse for more advanced jumping competitions you will need a number of suitable fences which comply with safety regulations. A suitable location – indoor school or outdoor manège – is also essential. Out of doors one should also have some natural fences and

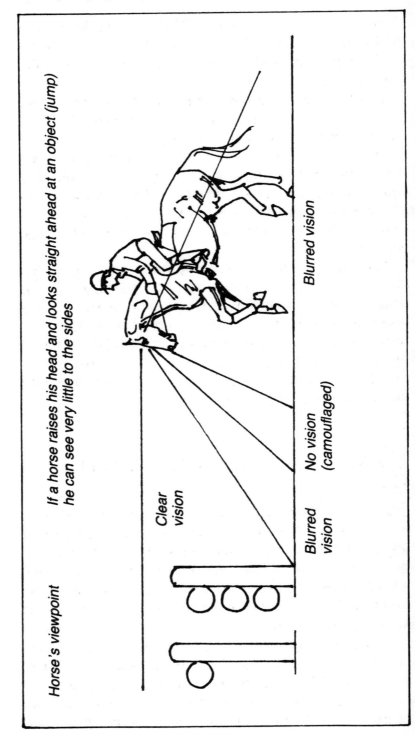

Horse's viewpoint

If a horse raises his head and looks straight ahead at an object (jump) he can see very little to the sides

Clear vision

Blurred vision

No vision (camouflaged)

Blurred vision

Blurred vision

several water jumps of varying width. The following are the different types of fence:

Straight (upright) fences Wall, gate, palisade
Spread fences Oxer (parallel) triple bar (over water)
Natural obstacles Bank, drop

The building of fences is explained in detail in many publications. In general you have to try and look at a fence with a horse's eyes, which are situated at the sides of his head and are constructed differently from the human eye, providing him with almost all-round horizontal vision, but making it difficult for him to fix his eye on an object straight in front of him.

This necessitates two factors in the building of fences: the obstacle has to have (1) a well defined ground line to help the horse to judge the take-off point, and (2) a clearly visible top line so that he can assess what height he has to jump. The higher the fence, the more important these two factors become.

In schooling, the horse's eye can be trained by using a take-off pole, but later on he will have to learn to jump without it.

Compact and well-filled fences induce the horse to jump higher and to respect the fence, but again the horse has to learn eventually to cope with thin, lightly built fences.

Training fences should be sturdy and should not fall too easily, as then the horse will not bother to jump carefully. On the other hand they should not be too solid, as this could cause an accident. The colour of a fence must stand out from that of the background colour. Therefore distinctive and varying colours – such as black and white and blue and yellow poles, and red and white wall sections – are especially important for high fences.

There are two different sequences of obstacles: combinations and related distances. Two or more fences with one or two non-jumping strides between the elements are called a *combination*. Three or more non-jumping strides of a given number between two obstacles are called a *related distance*.

The rider must be well informed about all distances and must know how a horse is likely to cope with them. The length of a horse's stride varies, depending on the horse's size, his degree of training, the speed at which he is going, the condition of the ground, etc. Therefore only very average measurements can be given. Similar considerations have to be made when giving take-off and landing points for various types and heights of fences.

On average, the horse's canter stride is 3.50 metres long. If the horse lands 2 metres behind the fence, the rider can then measure from this point how many strides his horse would need up to the take-off point at the next fence. A distance between two fences of 17.50 to 18 metres would mean four non-jumping strides. The horse could cover 21.50 to 22 metres in five non-jumping strides. Longer distances between fences would not be considered to be a related distance, and the next fence would have to be approached as a single fence.

The following are some nominal distances between two fences (normal distances):

Number of non-jumping strides	*Distance in metres*
3	14 – 15
4	17.50 – 18.50
5	21 – 22
6	24.50 – 25.50
7	28 – 29

When training for open jumping competitions, to start with the related distances should be suitable for the individual horse, but gradually both horse and rider should learn to negotiate the different distances used in competition.

An open show jumper is trained to improve not only his jumping but also his manoeuvrability and his ability to gallop. Both of these aspects must be developed during the horse's flat training and while jumping. The trainer must consider this when designing the line of a training course, as well as the fact that he will have to incorporate changes of direction. The training venue and the going also have to be changed occasionally. If a horse is trained only on sand he might be handicapped when having to compete on grass.

Any excess stress or strain in training must be avoided. The line of a course and the measurements of the fences must conform with the horse's standard of training. For example, extremely sharp turns can put a strain on the horse's joints.

3. Training

Training a show jumping horse to advanced level means a two- to three-year course of intensive schooling which is supported and complemented by dressage training. In this course the horse's basic training is brought on and improved. His jumping ability is developed and then maintained. With correct education and suitable training a horse can remain in top form until old age.

3 (1) Training a Show Jumping Horse for Open Competition

The principal factor in advanced show jumping training is the ability to jump big fences. This involves acquiring the necessary confidence, as well as the physical and psychological preparation.

The horse gains confidence by successfully completing daily training, but jumping only carefully built fences of medium height and difficulty does not provide him with the necessary routine. For this reason the demands have sometimes to be increased so that they are close to the limit of the horse's ability. Also his endurance has to be improved. Jumping ability alone does not make a winner; the horse must also have stamina. The heart, lungs and circulation can only be improved and maintained by daily exercise. Without neglecting walk and trot, most of the work is in canter.

The rider has to check all the time that the impulsion from the quarters goes 'through the back' into a soft but definite contact with the mouth. A show jumper is ridden with the head and neck in a deeper, rounder outline than a dressage horse to ensure that the back is working.

Equally important is the horse's obedience to the

rider's forward-driving leg aid and he must be ready to lengthen or shorten his stride instantly. A flying change must be executed promptly. Jumping from turns must be practised. The horse's manoeuvrability must be constantly improved.

A large part of training will consist of jumping combinations of different types with varying distances and approached from all angles.

Faulty technique, stiffness in the back, lack of bascule, bad leg movement, etc, are corrected through dressage and gymnastic jumping and by using combinations of a special design, as will be explained later.

Apart from training, however, the horse's ability to negotiate a big fence is all-important. The rider cannot always be absolutely spot-on in his judgement of the take-off point and might be out by half a metre here and there. The horse's jumping ability is then needed to make up the difference.

Not only during training but also in competition the horse must be relaxed. To achieve this he needs to be 'entertained' and interested, with a lot of variation in his work. It might be advisable to take him out twice daily – maybe with another rider – just to give him enough and varied exercise.

3 (2) Dressage Gymnastics for the Show Jumping Horse

In top-class jumping competitions a fraction of a second is often the winning factor, and here the well schooled, obedient horse always has the advantage. This is why in training an advanced show jumping horse the dressage also has to advance.

It is advisable to practise jumping dressage around fences in the jumping arena or manège. Like the dressage horse, the show jumper starts his daily work with relaxing exercises – also aiming for '*Rhythm – Losgelassenheit – Contact*'. But in contrast to the dressage horse the show jumper is worked in a deeper outline. He does not have to have the same degree of collection, therefore he cannot – or does not need to – have the same elevated outline. As mentioned previously, the lower outline will encourage the back to work and bascule, but this desirable rounding and stretching of neck and back muscles must not be forced by the use of auxiliary reins. Only horses with extremely difficult conformation – badly set head, short neck with heavy underneck muscles – may justify temporary use of running reins (mainly as a timesaving effort).

Of course it is not possible to lay down hard and fast rules on how to work an advanced horse on the flat, but in general the daily work should be started by walking on a long rein. Then work on frequent transitions, trot-canter-trot, on long and moderately curved lines. In addition the occasional use of trotting poles, and/or riding out, adds variety to the relaxing period. Extra work on the flat would aim to achieve better obedience to the leg aids, improved 'Durchlässigkeit', straightness and some collection.

Leg obedience is important for every riding horse, but especially for a show jumper, as the rider with his short stirrups cannot use his lower leg as efficiently as a dressage rider with long stirrups.

Various exercises improve leg obedience, depending on the horse's stage of schooling. These are: turn on the forehand, leg-yielding and other lateral work, turn around the haunches, and frequent variations within the paces, which for a show jumper are especially important. In trot as well as in canter the horse must lengthen and shorten his stride instantly from the slightest aid. The actual quality of the medium and extended paces need not be the same as in dressage, but the transitions must take place *instantly*; in a split second the full pushing power must be available and under control.

A show jumper must accept a good contact especially on the outside rein. Working the horse with a slight inwards flexion – always making sure that the neck is straight and secure in front of the shoulders – brings him more on to the outside rein, especially if well supported by the inside leg and an elastically yielding inside rein. Only when the horse is safely on the outside rein can the rider make tight turns at a faster speed.

A strong contact or pulling on the inside rein brings the horse on to the outside shoulder and carries him out of the turn. The outside rein, however, will only work if the horse is straight. Only when the hind legs follow in the track of the forelegs can the horse use their pushing power and impulsion economically. When a horse goes crooked the rider's rein actions cannot influence the quarters but get stuck in the poll, and the power from the horse's hind-quarters escapes sideways. Therefore the horse's straightness has to be worked on and improved all the time, especially at this advanced level. Exercises used for straightening the horse are riding on curved lines, continuously changing direction, and lateral work, especially shoulder-in. The lateral movements are ridden in a shortened trot, alternating with lengthened strides on straight lines and canter work on circles. Counter-canter also helps to straighten the horse, because the horse turns against the direction of the canter and thus gives the rider an opportunity to become more active with the outside aids. Turns around the haunches and pirouettes introduce some collection into dressage work; a higher degree of collection is not necessary for a show jumper.

It is important for a show jumper to be supple in the haunches and light in the forehand, so that he moves in balance and has 'spring'. The straightness and some degree of collection will enable the horse also to make a flying change when changing direction without any loss of time. The 'accidental' flying changes which a horse sometimes shows in the field or in tight turns often unbalance him so that he continues in disunited canter. Such changes do not save time and can be hard on the horse's legs. Even if a rider accepts them in the beginning

101

he should during further training gradually revert to orthodox changes out of a certain degree of collection and asked for with correct aids. The aids are given with the new outside leg and new outside rein, only very little with the weight, and hardly any movement of the rider's upper body, as this unbalances the horse.

Before finishing daily work on the flat there should be some relaxing exercises: cantering on a large circle and allowing the horse to stretch his nose forwards and downwards, then shortening the reins and riding him up to the bit again. Repeating this exercise six to ten times makes the horse relaxed and improves his ability to use his back. Between all the suppling work on the flat it is important to ride forward in forward seat position, at times without stirrups, to improve the rider's balance. Use long lines across the whole training area, turning around fences, etc. Do not ride only along the wall or familiar tracks.

At the end of each session the horse should be walked on a long or loose rein.

3 (3) How to Develop and Improve Jumping Technique

It is assumed that a horse chosen for advanced training has experience in novice competitions and is jumping fences of about 1.20 metres even at a higher speed. The experience needed for advanced competitions can only be obtained by jumping higher fences. This in turn is hard on the horse's legs, and must therefore be carried out very carefully and in moderation. The fences used have to be built progressively and correctly for the purpose, and the horse should be well warmed up, though not tired.

The difficulty of jumping higher fences usually lies in finding the correct take-off point. The rider must be able to judge the take-off point from some distance away, and must shorten or lengthen the horse's stride accordingly and with the least effort. The horse has to be very responsive and should react in a split second.

Various factors influence the location of the correct take-off point. Among them are:
☐ The type of fence.
☐ The going.
☐ The speed of the approach.
☐ The height of the fence.
☐ The horse's individual style of jumping.
The more the rider learns to assess these factors and to ride accordingly the more permanent will be his success.

If an ordinary upright fence is approached at a basic speed the best take-off point will be as far in front of the ground line as the height of the fence. If approached at a faster speed the horse should stand back a little further. If the speed is too fast the horse will most likely flatten and then knock the fence. When approaching a fair-sized water jump the horse should take off close to the front edge of the water in order to make the width.

A horse's performance is influenced by the going. In deep going the horse sinks in and has to jump that much higher, requiring more power from behind. Good going also influences the horse's method of jumping. The rider therefore has to assess the situation and to adjust his basic speed, which must be such that the rider is able to push. Horses who pick their own speed and rush into fences do not allow the rider to push, and he therefore cannot ride for the correct take-off point. It is a matter of luck whether the fence is cleared or not.

On the other hand the rider must never surprise the horse with his aids when riding to the take-off point. It would irritate him and ruin his confidence. The best way is to train the horse correctly, and during this time he will gradually get used to the rider's aids and will wait confidently for him to ride into the fence.

A good show jumper has courage to jump higher fences, and the rider has to improve and maintain this courage. This means that a rider has to adjust a little to the horse's individual way of jumping.

To teach horse and rider to find the correct take-off

point for a higher fence, a placing fence (low) is used, two canter strides in front of the higher fence. The distance should be suitable for the individual horse. The placing fence regulates the approach to the higher fence and gives rider and horse confidence.

Another method is to place at the desired take-off place two poles on the ground in V-formation, the point of the V towards the fence.

To teach the take-off and to make the horse a little more careful, poles can be placed on the ground parallel to the fence in front of and behind it. For the approach to an initially 1-metre high upright fence at a trot, the pole is placed on the ground 2.50 metres in front of the fence. The horse should approach the pole in trot. Then with each jump the fence is raised according to the standard of the horse. He must remain in trot over the pole even when the fence is higher.

When carrying out the same exercise in canter the pole is placed at a distance of 3 metres in front of the fence. If poles are placed on the ground behind the fence to teach the horse to 'come back' to the rider they should be at a distance of 3 to 3.50 metres when jumped from a trot; when the fence is jumped from canter the pole on the ground behind it should be at 3.50 metres or more.

If jumping from trot the rider does not use rising trot but a 'light sitting trot', with the weight on his thighs. In canter the approach speed is a little slower than at a fence which has no pole on the ground in front or behind.

If a horse does not bascule well enough, use two upright fences 7 metres apart, with a pole on the ground centred between the two fences. This will encourage the horse to 'look' and lower his outline.

Tight distances between fences make the horse alert and quick to pick up his legs.

Bascule and leg technique can be improved by jumping an oxer with two poles in V-formation in front of the fence, sloping upwards, with the point of the V at the centre on top of the front oxer pole. Another method is to widen the oxer and place the pole diagonally across the top.

As a rule, the rider must concentrate on the approach and maintain a steady contact with the horse's mouth. He should not drop the reins nor pull them backwards. Over the fence his hands should move forward in the direction of the mouth to allow the horse to bascule. If on the approach the rider is aware that he will meet the fence correctly he can then ease the reins a stride sooner.

3 (4) Approaching and Jumping Combinations and Water

When approaching and jumping combinations the actual dimensions are as important as the horse's way of going and jumping. The rider has to rely considerably on his eye, his feel and his experience.

With combinations, the approach is most important. Although advice often given is to concentrate always on the last part of a combination, this is only true in that the rider should concentrate on every fence that he jumps. If he misses the correct take-off point at the first part of a combination it will be of little use to concentrate on the last part. To clear a combination the most important point is to get into it correctly, which means finding the correct take-off point for the first part and reaching it at the correct speed and angle.

In the case of combinations with one or two non-jumping strides between elements it is important to know whether the distance is short or long. From this knowledge the rider decides whether or not to get close to the first element in the approach. Any shortening or lengthening of stride during the approach has to be carried out without loss of rhythm, and early enough for the final stride to accumulate power for the take-off and for it to end *exactly* at the spot where the horse should take off. It is wrong to break the even rhythm and suddenly to increase speed during the last few strides before take-off.

Even though it is true that some expert riders on horses with which they are well acquainted can use this approach technique, it should not be common practice. It is correct and desirable to approach any fence at an even, basic pace without any change in rhythm.

The best line of approach is usually a straight line vertically towards the middle of the fence. In training, however, the horse should also be taught to approach on a more diagonal line and from turns. This helps the rider to learn how the horse will react if he ever has to ride such a line in competition. It also gives him the chance to lengthen the distance in a tight combination by riding through it on a diagonal line.

In training, the jumping of combinations can be improved by placing poles on the ground between the elements. This helps the horse to regulate the non-jumping strides and the rider to feel the rhythm of the non-jumping strides. Combinations with two non-jumping strides are more difficult than those with one non-jumping stride, the reason being that the rider has little influence over the first of the two non-jumping strides, which often makes such a combination seem rather short. Such a combination should therefore be approached with special care.

In jumping water the problem is not the spread of the water jump – because even in top class competition it is only a little more than a normal canter stride – but the colour and movement of the water. The same factors apply for a water jump as for any other fence. The approach is the deciding factor, and many riders approach a water jump incorrectly. It does not need a long approach, but a little more speed and impulsion than for an upright fence, while the same basic rhythm is maintained. The canter stride should become longer and more powerful, but the rhythm should not become faster. It is also wrong to approach water at a canter which is too slow and lacks impulsion.

Training over water jumps should be started with a

small amount of water which has a fence over it as camouflage. The width of the water is gradually increased and the camouflage is decreased until the bare water with a brush in front is arrived at.

If a horse shows a tendency to fault at water – to step into it or to step short – use a pole over the last third of the water. The colour of this pole should stand well out from the background.

The rider will find it more difficult to follow the movement over a water jump than over an ordinary fence. He must therefore make sure that in the approach the horse is 'together', and must not allow him to become long.

4. Riding in a Competition

Competing at a higher level is physically as well as psychologically demanding for the horse. Participation has therefore to be carefully planned in order to save the horse's resources. It is also important to choose a type of competition appropriate to the standard of training and suitability of the horse.

Competing at the correct frequency in competitions of the right nature will mature the horse, but too much and the wrong type of competition will discourage him, set him back in his training and ruin his health. There are, for instance, temperamental horses, or scopey horses who have not yet learned to gallop. Neither type would be suited to competitions in which they have to gallop to win. They should rather be used in competitions where their jumping ability counts and not the speed. On the other hand, a horse who is especially fast and manoeuvrable but has limited jumping ability would not be suited to such a class. As their experience grows, horses often develop in such a way that later on they can be used successfully in competitions to which they were unsuited earlier.

On the whole a horse is only ready to compete after he has shown at home in training that his ability has reached the relevant standard. The show ground is not a training place. It can be used for experience, but faults must always be eradicated at home.

4 (1) Preparing for a Competition

Warming up determines the standard of performance in the ring. It prepares the horse to be at his best and draws his attention to the fences.

A calm and concentrated warming-up is better than a

short, rushed session. Its extent will depend on the horse's needs. Lazy horses need only short, sharp exercise. Such horses should be ridden forward and 'woken up'. Temperamental, excitable horses need a longer warming–up period, and they must be calmed down until they allow the rider to push. It is also advisable to give excitable horses a separate work-out, before the actual warming-up for the competition. It is, of course, an extra demand to work a horse a couple of times per day, but it pays off by producing a relaxed animal for the competition.

To warm up the horse, simple trot and canter movements are ridden as when training at home. This is the most important part of the warming-up, because here the rider must achieve total 'Losgelassenheit', total relaxation and unrestrained movement of all joints. By giving and retaking the reins in canter the rider can check the progress of this work. Once 'Losgelassenheit' is achieved the rider progresses to the canter, using the whole arena, with frequent changes of rein, and with some flying changes. If the horse is listening and 'losgelassen' you can start with some practice jumps. It would be totally wrong to jump continuously and without a plan, or to start jumping right from the beginning.

When jumping practice fences, again the horse's peculiarities have to be considered. Some horses need practice jumps just before entering the ring. Others need a long break between jumping the practice fence and starting a round. The important factor is for the horse to enter the arena breathing normally; an exhausted horse with heaving flanks is never going to jump at its best. On the other hand, the horse should not get cold after the warming-up. The practice jumps should make him alert for the competition, and should warm up all his muscles and joints. It is wrong to use the practice arena as a schooling ground.

A few jumps over different types of fences should be sufficient. In the practice arena the jumps should not be higher than the standard of the competition. Only before a puissance competition should higher fences be jumped.

In the practice arena there are never more than just a few poles available, so start over a low vertical, then a small oxer, which is higher behind. After more flat work the oxer is made into a parallel, and jumped. If the horse will not 'open out' over the jump, finish the warm-up over an oxer. If, however, the horse rushes his fences, finish with a vertical.

Every fence should be approached with the horse well under control and on the aids. Riders who have to use auxiliary reins – especially running reins – in the warming-up arena, have not done their homework. The only auxiliary that may be used is the running martingale. The argument that horses who were warmed up with running reins won the competition is misleading. The forceful effect of the running rein fades away after the first few fences of the course. The fight then starts, and having to fight costs nerves and energy, which will mean the horse being worn out more quickly.

Another bad habit is using the practice fence to give the horse a 'reminder', by purposely approaching the fence incorrectly and placing the horse so close that he hits it. As a rule, such treatment shows lack of correct preparation at home, and generally does not pay off.

Should the horse accidentally make a mistake over the practice fence and knock himself, a lower, easier fence should be jumped, to make sure that he is not frightened and is still willing to take it on. If the horse hesitates and is tense, help him regain his confidence by jumping more low fences.

When the warming-up is finished, do not stand around. If you want to watch the other competitors jump, do so while still keeping the horse on the move.

As important as the warming-up for a competition is the cooling off afterwards. If this is carried out incorrectly it is a bad start for the next class or the next round. After going through the finish the horse should be brought back to trot or walk and taken out of the arena immediately. After the girths have been loosened he should be taken to a quiet part of the show ground and walked on a long rein until he breathes normally again and is cooled off.

Both horse and rider must be well prepared for a competition. An unfit rider is slow in his reactions and is a burden to the best trained horse. To ride several rounds in an open class the rider has to be fit as well as prepared mentally. Before warming up the horse you should have studied the course plan to find out about all the important points of the competition: start and finish line, compulsory course line or flags, time allowed, jump-off course, etc.

Walking the course is very important. Take a close look at every fence. Examine the ground in front and behind the fence. And while walking, follow exactly the line you intend to ride. If time is a deciding factor, you must walk and memorise short cuts. All distances should be walked, measured and related to the horse's stride, whether this is long or short. How to approach a combination or how many strides to take in a related distance must be decided. You must know and memorise the fact that a combination with two non-jumping strides probably rides shorter than it measures. The line of the jump-off course must also be walked, and possible short cuts evaluated.

Every competitor knows how important concentration is before a class, and how easily a competition can be lost if one small detail goes wrong.

4 (2) Training between Competitions

A horse might be given a break after a show weekend or at the end of the season with the best of intentions, but this rest can be disastrous for him. Even a fully trained older horse needs a set training programme between shows in order to stay healthy and fit. The type of programme depends on the timespan between shows.

If the last show did not pose a problem, work until the

next one can be designed just to maintain fitness. Plenty of canter work is needed, as well as ordinary relaxing and suppling exercises. The rider has to improve the horse's suppleness in canter and his overall obedience. Older horses also need some jumping between shows to keep them in competition spirit and condition. Without jumping practice show jumpers get stiff, and this is evident when they are ridden again after the short break.

For jumping training between shows gymnastic jumping is used to save the horse's legs. Medium-high single fences at various related distances are recommended.

If in the competition there were any problems at a certain type of fence – perhaps at a combination or obstacles at a related distance – work to eliminate these problems before the next show. Demands are minimised and dressage is used to ensure that the foundation work is in order. After you are certain that the difficulties can be tackled at a reduced level, demands can then be increased once or twice up to competition level to give the horse confidence.

If there is a longer break between competitions the horse might be let out to grass – but training should be resumed, slowly and carefully, before the next competition.

5. Working Difficult and Spoiled Show Jumpers

The rider who contemplates re-training a spoiled horse has to answer two questions:

☐ Why is the horse difficult? Are there conformation faults which make it unrealistic to spend a long time re-training the horse?

☐ Does the rider, or trainer, have the necessary experience and temperament to do this work successfully?

Only when the rider can answer both these questions positively should he start on the horse in question.

The various reasons for difficulties with a show jumper need analysis.

First let us consider the pulling, rushing horse. He definitely needs a calm, quiet rider with a lot of feel and 'tact'. The reason for a horse pulling or rushing is usually that he feels pain, mostly in the back. To correct this, strengthen the back through lungeing. The horse must carry his head and neck deeper and arch his back in a 'fresh' working trot and canter. These will strengthen the back muscles and enable the horse later on to make use of his full ability.

At first a spoiled horse should be jumped only very little, and the work should be directed forwards giving him self-confidence and making him stronger. When starting to jump, the fences should at first be inviting. Well presented single fences about 1 metre high can be jumped from trot. After the jump the horse is brought back to trot as soon as possible – if necessary by going on to a circle. He should be completely settled before approaching another fence. If other horses are working in the arena, ride often on the opposite rein to the other horses. After the daily session take the horse for a hack, or ride out to calm him down further.

Lazy horses are much easier to re-train, and to get them thinking forward it is often sufficient to give them a good gallop with other horses. All the same, the rider should try to find out why the horse does not want to go forward. If stable management or feeding are the reason, these must be corrected. A veterinary inspection with blood tests, etc, should be arranged.

Other difficulties, such as stopping at a fence or refusing to enter the arena or to pass the exit, etc, are caused by bad experiences. The horse probably hurt himself at a fence or the rider made a bad mistake, either in a competition or in training.

If the horse hurts himself at a certain fence he might subsequently refuse at this type of fence. It should then be practised at a very reduced height, until the horse feels safe and confident. It might even be advisable to give the frightened animal a lead with another horse. Only after he has gained confidence at the fence and in the rider should the height be raised gradually. It is important for this work not to be rushed: experience shows that if it *is*, the horse will quickly revert to his bad habits.

Horses who refuse a long way from the fence, veer sideways and try to get out of control are very unpleasant. In this case it is best to stop jumping altogether and to improve the horse's training on the flat. A strong, positive rider should work the horse and get him under control, so that he goes forward into both reins. Only when the horse is going straight and listening to the aids should jumping be started again, and initially over very small fences. After a jump, before approaching the next fence it is important to ensure that the horse is under control again and 'listening'. Such horses are often not straight enough and tend to break away to the same side. It is therefore helpful to bring the outside hind leg – which tries to escape sideways – well in line by means of sideways driving leg aids and strong support of the outside rein, so that the approach to the fence can be absolutely straight. The jumping whip on the outside shoulder gives support. In a

114

competition, avoid riding against the clock as this kind of horse would tend to use the faster speed to run out of control again.

Older, experienced horses sometimes begin to stand back or run too close to their fences without any obvious reason. It may be that their nerves are deteriorating or that their forelegs are beginning to become tender, which makes them afraid of landing after the fence. The cure for this is rather time-consuming, as the horse needs to be rested to refresh his nerves and legs. If it is intended not to write off the horse totally but to use him again in competition later on, he will have to be worked over fences now and again, even during the rest period. Otherwise his muscles will deteriorate and become too weak. A total lay-off can cause more serious health problems when the horse goes back into work.

In general it can be said that in re-schooling spoiled horses it is most important to build fences which are inviting and easy to jump. Keep demands minimal and take care not to overface the horse at any stage, as this will cause more disobedience and a setback in progress.

6. Tips on How to Keep a Show Jumper Fit for Competition

To follow a systematic and basic dressage training is the requisite for the health, fitness and willingness of a competition horse – no matter in which discipline he specialises. The rider, too, must have undergone the same basic training.

Only a horse who is constantly listening to the rider's aids and who has had a logical and systematic training is balanced and 'durchlässig' enough to last for years in competition, without suffering any wear and tear.

A badly or unschooled horse is not 'durchlässig', and he fights his rider constantly, using up his resources. The result is overall exhaustion. Heart and lungs can be damaged permanently and the horse is prone to certain bone diseases, as well as tendon and muscle problems. He may stumble, change legs constantly, miss the correct take-off point, resist when making turns, knock himself, hurt himself at fences and be unable to land softly after a fence. The whole bone, tendon and muscle structure suffers all kinds of injuries.

A correctly trained and relaxed horse can be ridden carefully and according to plan. His energy can be regulated. He can be collected easily and turned in balance, and he can be ridden on a light contact to the utmost of his ability without harming his health and wellbeing. The rider also stays relaxed, full of energy, and in constant control. However, any healthy and well-schooled horse can be ruined quite quickly – healthwise and performance wise – if handed over to a worse rider with less feel and bad nerves.

All this makes one point clear: to keep a horse sound and in top condition for high performance competitions, horse and rider must have a sound dressage training. But this alone is not enough. In addition, the right type of horse must have been chosen from the beginning. A horse who is soft by nature will not stand up to the strain of top class competition, even if all the other conditions are right. Therefore only a horse who has remained sound throughout his upgrading should be trained for top-class competition.

It is also essential for there to be a confident relationship between the horse and his rider and/or groom. The most perfect training system is useless if the horse is not kept mentally in good condition. All guidelines are valueless if the horse becomes nervous, if he turns sour or becomes a coward, and if he does not work willingly.

The groom plays a big part in keeping a horse physically and mentally in good condition. Peak fitness can only be achieved if the horse is content and receives the best of care without being pampered. A warning signal is if a horse stops eating, although this can be due to illness, teeth or worms as well as to a little too much training.

To sum up, the deciding factors in keeping a horse in top competition form are not just medical care but much more the basic training, built up logically and systematically and the establishment of a trusting relationship between horse and rider. Correct training improves the horse's health, and conditions him in various ways: blood circulation is improved, new blood cells are formed, and with increased circulation there is improved excretion of the toxins in the body. The cleansing of all tissue fluids increases the body's resistance against disease and weaknesses. All actions which decrease blood circulation should be avoided. These include bandages which shrink when the horse is sweating, constant cold hosing of the legs, or frequent use of poudre Amoricaine which also dries out the skin.

Regular movement improves the density of bone tissue and stabilises tendons, increasing their carrying power. Muscles are built up and hardened. Progressive training in conjunction with appropriate feeding and stable management will prepare the horse for competition and ensure that he stays sound under pressure. In case of illness or injury, diagnosis and treatment must be left to a veterinary surgeon who specialises in horses. Amateurs experimenting can lead to irreparable damage.

After a hard competition or a long season the horse must be let down gradually. A sudden change cuts off the support derived from regular work, which means that the horse will be vulnerable.

The most common problems in competition horses are injuries to the legs, and wind, heart and circulation trouble.

Leg problems, such as swollen joints, navicular disease, ringbone and spavins are mostly due to irregular work or too much training. Stress is also put on the legs by carrying too much weight or making sharp, unbalanced turns. Tendon trouble can be due to too fast a speed or too much jumping, as well as to external injury. Heart and circulation problems, broken wind, colic and chronic bronchitis usually stem from bad stable management or from the horse being worked too soon after an illness.

For navicular disease, which is common in show jumpers, preventive measures are, firstly, correct shoeing in relation to the horse's anatomy and, secondly, the correct riding of turns. Very sharp turns at high speed should be ridden with the outside rein and inside leg. Pulling on the inside rein when turning puts too much stress on to the forefoot.

SECTION THREE
Guidelines for Event Training

1. Introduction

Top-class three-day event riding is often considered the most valuable branch of competition riding. The various phases of the competition are demanding, and training a horse for eventing involves much time and knowledge. For the actual competition the rider must have a very clear mind and plenty of 'heart'. Success means recognition and reward for the endeavour of both horse and rider.

A three-day event is important not only for the competitor but also for the breeder as it is a test of all physical and psychological requirements in a modern warmblood horse. The results allow the breeder to make decisions about the breeding value of certain blood lines. Mares and stallions who have competed successfully in three-day events have often produced equally successful offspring.

The guidelines given here are based on facts and experiences which have been gathered before and after World War II at national and international level. We are giving only the basic principles and will not go into detail concerning different methods, schools, training yards or events.

Guidelines such as these are well justified, as nowadays everyone has to look for ways to suit their own particular situation.

2. The Event Horse and Rider

2 (1) The Horse

Because training a horse for three-day events takes years, you have to chose the right material, otherwise time and money will be wasted.

For one-day events almost any warmblood horse is suitable, as long as he is sound, has had a good basic training and is fit and in good condition. One-day events, however, are merely a stepping stone for the three-day competition and choosing a horse should therefore be done with the latter in mind.

The cross-country phase is a test of endurance, speed, courage and jumping ability, so a three-quarter bred horse or a sturdy Thoroughbred – sound, with a good, bold temperament – is suitable. A horse of medium height with good conformation and balance is best. During his initial training period he should show good temperament, light-footed movement and above average jumping ability. He should be able to gallop and should show no tendency to tendon trouble, as these are two factors which cannot be influenced by training.

Horses with bad temperaments should not be considered, as they take too long to train, are detrimental to the rider's nerve, and all too often let the rider down in a difficult situation in competition.

2 (2) Training

During a high-performance test as demanded in a three-day event the horse can only save energy, legs and joints if his three paces are supple, relaxed, rhythmical and balanced. A horse who has been made supple and elastic through dressage training is always under control and obedient, and can carry his rider energy-efficiently across difficult country.

This dressage training does not include as high a degree of collection as for a dressage horse, but the carrying power of the eventer's quarters must be well developed, so that the horse's forehand is lightened, thus saving front tendons and joints. It will also prevent the horse from pulling and lying on the rider's hand.

In *The Principles of Riding* we gave advice on how to train the young horse. This is also valid for three-day events, but training an eventer is a long term process. The young horse starts his basic training at the age of three and a half and after one year he should be at preliminary level in dressage and jumping. At the same time, riding across country on a long rein is all important. The horse should be worked in hilly countryside in the company of other horses or alone and should be made familiar with dry ditches, water, banks and uneven going. This will make him 'clever' and surefooted.

Training must proceed with calmness and patience. Correct basic training, together with the horse's growing trust in his rider, are the best foundation for the development of a future competitor.

In jumping and cross-country training especially the trainer has to take his time, keeping demands low at the beginning and later raising them very gradually. A situation should never be allowed to arise which could cause resistance by the horse. If he begins to show resistance or unwillingness, though neither trainer nor rider is at fault, it could be a sign that the horse is not suitable and he should be tried in another riding discipline.

As a five-year-old the horse can compete in a novice class at a one-day event, as long as he has shown in training that he is fit and ready. The horse must be at least six years old before competing in a three-day event.

3. The Event Rider

Any rider can compete in a one-day event, once he has completed basic training on the flat and over jumps, has mastered the forward seat, and has enough courage to gallop over fences across country.

Riders aiming to compete in a full three-day event must be as tough and fit as their horses. They should have strong nerves, stamina and powers of concentration. On the other hand they must also be sensitive and have an understanding of the horse which enables them to save his energy reserves. A stiff rider with unsympathetic hands has as negative an influence in eventing as in every other sphere of riding.

The rider's weight is also important. The minimum weight to be carried by all senior competitors in the endurance test of an international three-day event is 75kg, including, if necessary, all saddlery and equipment carried by the horse except the bridle. Riders exceeding the limit by four or five kilos or more are generally not suitable for this kind of event.

Only a rider who competes because he loves the sport, and not because he loves winning or because of eventual financial rewards, will enjoy eventing. He must have the right approach to it, be willing to work hard, and be self-critical. He must learn from every mistake made and try to improve himself constantly. The talented rider who is always eager to learn will do well in international or even Olympic competitions.

Because an eventer has only very few chances to compete each year, the rider has few chances to learn about ringcraft. He should therefore compete as often as possible in other disciplines. Good training for the rider would be some racing, either on the flat or over fences.

4. Preparing a Horse for Competition

4 (1) Training

The purpose of training is to prepare a horse so that he goes to the start in peak condition, and competes to the best of his ability without any ill effect on his confidence, health or nerves.

As already mentioned, we shall give only the basic principles for training. They should guide the trainer and rider in making their own programme according to individual possibilities. Deviations may be necessary for various reasons – such as the horse's condition – and the sensible rider has to assess them every single day.

Well planned, consistent work which is adjusted to any given situation is better than adhering to a rigid schedule, as this could cause serious harm. The basic knowledge gained from German riding experience is explained in these guidelines. Together with the rider's own personal experience, it will help him to work out a training programme.

To compete in a one-day event a special fitness programme over four to six weeks is necessary. For a three-day event the *minimum* is eight weeks.

Before beginning this training the horse must be sound and in normal riding condition. If he is not in work but has had time off, the recommended time span has to be extended accordingly. The more the fitness training is spread out timewise, the less strenuous it will be for the horse and the more stable his condition.

The degree of difficulty in eventing necessitates a long-term training programme. From the beginning the horse must have already achieved the fitness and experience of a novice dressage horse or show jumper. He should also have had some cross-country experience.

As well as normal work, fitness training should also include an additional period of one to two hours of exercise without stress – such as walk on a long rein, being led, or being turned out at grass. This additional exercise will not be boring for the horse. If carried out systematically over a period of time it will result in a marked strengthening of his legs.

The first event of the year needs especially careful preparation. If the event is in the spring the horse can start working out of doors as soon as the weather permits. The winter should have been spent improving the horse's dressage and overall obedience. Jumping should be practised, but only up to novice level; it is not the height of the fences but the style of jumping that is important.

A typical training plan for a week would be as follows:

Sunday
Take the horse for a long hack, walk and trot him on, on a long rein.

Monday and Thursday
Canter work on a large sand or grass area. On one of the two days, cantering can be replaced by walk and trot on hilly going.

Tuesday and Friday
Dressage training in different locations.

Wednesday
Flat work at canter in forward seat with short stirrups, gymnastic jumping over show jumps.

Saturday
Cross-country training.

More specific details are as follows:

Sunday
A relaxed ride out of at least two hours, at walk and trot. Its purpose is to relax the horse and soothe his nerves.

On all other days the horse should also be warmed up at walk and trot before the actual training session, and afterwards should be walked – outside – on a long rein for quite some time. This will soon have a positive influence on the horse's mental and physical condition.

Monday and Thursday

To condition the horse, canter work is essential, but it does need good going to prevent injuries. Especially when towards the end of the training period the horse has to gallop to clear his wind, uneven or deep going would be dangerous. The gallop (500 metres per minute) should only be ridden on a permanent race track which is in good condition, or on similar suitable going, whereas canter work can be ridden on an ordinary field, stubble or dirt track.

An appropriate speed course should be set up, with markers at the various distances. The trainer or assistant can most easily check the times if the course is marked out in a circle: e.g. a distance of 4000 metres at a speed of 400 metres per minute should take the rider exactly ten minutes.

The event rider should always wear and use the same watch as in competition, as it is important to be familiar with it.

Canter work is started at 350 metres per minute over a maximum 2000 metres. If the horse stays calm and light on the bit, in the second week the work can be increased to 400 metres per minute over a maximum 3000 metres. Any further increase will depend on the horse's progress in training and the type and conditions of the intended event.

When preparing for a three-day event the maximum work on a canter day is 8000 metres at 400 metres per minute. Whatever the distance, at half-way stage the rider should pull up gradually to a trot and change the rein.

As a pipe-opener, over two or three days towards the end of the training period the distance should be shortened and the speed increased to a maximum of 600 metres per minute, on good going. Before a three-day event this speed should have been achieved at the distance of Phase B of the intended competition.

An experienced, sensible rider/trainer will find the best ratio for his canter work. A common horse is more subject to nerves than a three-quarter bred or Thoroughbred horse.

If the rider does not have the use of good going for a gallop he will either have to take his horse to a location suitable for this type of work or he will have to keep the speed down but work over a longer distance.

For the gallop, the stirrups should be shortened two or three holes from jumping length, so that they are five or six holes shorter than in dressage. A firm leg position with supple hip joints is as important as a firm contact on the outside rein.

Before any canter work is started the horse should, of course, be warmed up for thirty minutes in walk and trot.

Correct 'pulling up' after the gallop is very important for the safety of the horse's legs. He must be straight and must canter into the rider's hand. Still in forward seat, the rider eases and increases the rein tension very gently, using a soothing voice, and slows down the pace very gradually until the horse finally trots (rider in rising trot) and then pulls up to a walk. The rider then gives the reins completely.

When being prepared for a three-day event the horse must also learn to jump steeplechase fences. He should be started at show jumping speed over some simple brush fences, and the pace should gradually be increased. He should be ridden energetically forward with a deep hand which should never act backwards. Thus the horse will learn to stand back and gain ground in jumping.

It is wrong to jump steeplechase fences too often, as the horse will learn to hurdle his fences – which could be fatal for the cross-country phase and the show jumping.

During the canter work, heart and respiration rates should be measured, as they indicate the progress made in fitness and any other changes in the horse's body. Every trainer must be able to measure these rates in a very simple fashion. They should first be measured at rest (in the stable before the horse is taken out), immediately after the canter or gallop, and then during regression (while the horse is cooling off). Work conditions (speed, distance and condition of going) must be similar in order to make a comparison.

A mature eight-year-old horse should have a heart rate of 38 beats per minute. The heart-beat can be felt by placing the hand under the girth. Under stress (physical or mental) it can be three or four times as high. Under extreme stress it might even rise to six times the normal rate of rest.

About fifteen minutes after the canter work the heart rate should be normal again. Body temperature rises under stress by 1 to 4°C.

Respiration increases much more dramatically under stress. The number of breaths the horse takes per minute can be counted by watching his flank or nostrils. At rest the rate should be 8 to 12. Immediately after a canter or gallop this rate increases up to 80 to 100 per minute. This rate returns to normal more slowly than the heart rate.

Ten minutes after work a sufficiently fit horse should show no more than double his normal heart and respiration rates. Otherwise the stress has been too high or the horse is unfit.

On the whole it can be said that the better the horse's condition is through regular, slowly increasing work, the less the horse's heart and respiration rates and body temperature will rise during stress, and the quicker they will return to normal after work. It is advisable to keep a written record of all rates taken.

As already mentioned, one of the twice-weekly canter days can be replaced by walk and trot work in hilly countryside, if this is more suitable under local conditions or for any other reason. Hill work in light seat position is ideal to complement the fittening canter work as it puts strain on different tendons. How much of this work depends on the height of the hills, the degree of slope and the going. The rider has to be careful in assessing the degree of difficulty so as not to put too much strain on the horse.

Tuesday and Friday

The main aim of dressage work is constantly to improve, by use of the forward driving aids, the horse's basic training – the 'Losgelassenheit' – rhythm, contact (with a long neck), hindquarter activity and straightness.

When preparing for the FEI tests the horse's 'Durchlässigkeit' and lateral bend also have to be improved and some degree of collection has to be achieved in order to be able to perform the half-pass and counter-canter correctly.

The aim of dressage training is not only to ride the test correctly, but to improve the horse's overall obedience and agility, which in turn will improve his performance in the other phases of the competition.

It is not advisable to practise the whole test too often but to ride some of the movements whenever they fit into the various stages of the flat work session. The horse will then be alert and fresh in the test, and not mechanical as in a drill ride. For the same reason, in flat training it is important often to change the venue and the going from grass to sand or stubble.

Wednesday

On this day the agenda is aimed at flat work in the arena at canter in the forward seat, and at work over show jumps, culminating in a whole show jumping course.

The stirrups should be shortened three or four holes from dressage length. Work starts by walking the horse on a contact, followed by rising trot on circles and straight lines. The strike-off into the canter is first asked for on a circle in the dressage seat. If the horse stays on the bit and on the aids the rider should change to the forward seat. The horse should canter calmly in a constant rhythm and should stay on the bit and allow the rider to push. If the horse tries to lean on the bit the inside rein should be repeatedly yielded, and the voice should be used to calm the horse down.

If the horse canters working through his back and poll, and on a light contact, frequent changes between circles and straight lines on both reins can be used. To achieve complete harmony with the horse, the rider has to sit still and be supple – with springy joints and with still hands held deep beside and close to the horse's neck.

A longish canter session at moderate speed asks no effort of the horse if he remains calm. This sort of canter work teaches the horse to canter with the least output of energy across country and on the steeplechase track.

After an interval of fifteen to twenty minutes of walking on a loose rein, the jumping should begin.

First a few fences about 80cm high should be jumped from trot. Then three to six different fences up to 1.10 metres should be jumped from canter. Between fences the horse must maintain a calm, relaxed rhythm, well on the aids. During the last few strides of an approach the forward-driving aids should be slightly increased to encourage the horse to jump fluently.

Any backward movement of the rider's hands during the approach is a serious fault.

During the second half of the period this jumping training should consist of a full course of six to eight fences. The height of the fences should be up to 1.10 metres when preparing for a one-day event and up to 1.20 metres when preparing for a three-day event. In training it is important never to approach a fence unless the horse is well under control. This applies particularly to excitable horses who pull. Preparation on a circle with repeated yielding of the inside rein, and use of voice, help to prevent a horse rushing his fences. Only after harmony is re-established should the fence be approached again.

On alternate jumping days the jumping lane can be used. Constant changes between upright and spread fences and a varying number of non-jumping strides between the elements improve the horse's bascule and leg technique, as well as the rider's suppleness and ability to follow the movement.

As always, start with lowish fences at distances which are easy for the horse. The demands should be increased gradually to higher, more difficult fences and tighter and/ or longer distances between the elements. As always, finish the session while the horse is still going well.

Saturday

Work across country should be ridden with stirrups at jumping length and should start with relaxing walk and trot work followed by a quiet canter. Uneven going makes the horse surefooted – a vital asset for the cross-country phase. It also supples the horse in the same way as cavalletti. Hill work and jumping natural fences is next on the programme.

Ride up and down steep hills vertically to the slope and never diagonally, as this causes the horse to slip and also wears the joints in his legs. The rider makes the work easy for the horse by sitting forward with tight knees, the seat well out of the saddle, the hands deep and yielding so that the horse has freedom of the neck.

When training over cross-country fences drops require special attention. Many horses and riders feel uncomfortable when jumping drop fences but in one form or another they are part of every event. When training over drop fences it is important to give the horse confidence and never to force him over uninviting drops. Riding downhill is often a good preparation. Then a small upright is placed at the top, the middle or the bottom of the slope. Very slowly the demands should be increased.

The jump into water is handled in a similar fashion. By training over only moderately difficult water jumps horse and rider will learn to take them confidently in their stride. In training as well as in competition the rider should never risk a stop at this kind of fence. He should therefore approach every fence, however simple it may appear, with concentration and energy, so that the horse notices the rider's determination and jumps under all circumstances.

To ensure the rider's safety it is important for him never to be alone when training, as unforeseen situations might arise when he may need assistance. Another safety measure is for the rider always to wear a crash helmet, securely fastened. This is also the trainer's responsibility.

The training plan explained here should help the rider's understanding of a continuously escalating training programme. It should be based on as perfect conditions as are available, such as the facilities of a racecourse, or suitable country with hills and cross-country fences, though in reality the rider will often have to make do with less perfect conditions.

Every training programme should be individually planned. Sensitive horses have to be trained more carefully and more calmly than horses with good nerves, or even lazy horses who are inclined to get fat. It is up to the talent and understanding of the trainer to find the road to success.

The number of events that a horse can manage during a season varies with circumstances. Experience tells us that a sound, mature horse can tackle two or three three-day events and three or four one-day events per season, as long as he is not always ridden across country with winning in mind.

Between events part of the training plan is participation in medium dressage and the equivalent in show jumping competitions. Competing at a higher level nowadays requires specialised schooling, which is hardly of advantage to the eventer. Hunting between seasons can be of use as long as the horse does not become too hot. For excitable horses, hunting is not advisable.

Finally we must point out again that the main aim of training an eventer is the manifestation of mutual trust between horse and rider. Only then will there be a *team* willing to battle and to cope with the many difficult situations of an event.

4 (2) Stable Management (Feeding, Care and Shoeing)

Good stable management is as essential for an eventer as is good training.

The stable must be a well-ventilated loosebox which is quiet between feeding and working times. Automatic water is desirable, but if not available tap water should be given before each meal and late at night, especially on hot days.

A conscientious groom is the deciding factor for the horse's well-being. There must be a set stable routine, with the horse handled calmly but firmly; even in the stable he should be obedient.

The main diet should be top-quality oats or similar first-class concentrates, together with good meadow hay. Oats should be given whole, unless the horse has problem teeth. Whole oats supply more nourishment and force the horse to chew his feed, which improves saliva production and mastication. Carrots and linseed are valuable supplements, especially when the horse is changing his coat. Freshly-cut grass (not from the lawn mower) or a short daily grazing period improves digestion.

When in normal work an average of 4 to 5kg of oats should be sufficient. During fitness training the oats ration should be increased according to appetite. The horse should look forward to his feed and should eat up. If he loses appetite or if his coat loses its shine, overwork or organic disorder can be the cause. If he is overworked, the demands have to be reduced immediately, and nervous stress should especially be avoided.

Before a three-day event the normal feeding and watering routine should end five to six hours before the start, with a small feed.

Great care should be taken of the horse's feet. The legs

134

should be washed after exercise and the hooves should be greased. If possible, the same farrier should always be used. Full shoes are required during quiet work to give support and protection to the whole foot. For fast work and the competition itself shorter shoes should be fitted, to avoid their being pulled off. Of course for a three-day event the horse has to be shod all round. This should be done at least eight to ten days before the competition, and a good spare set of used shoes should be taken to the event. Studs are used for slippery going, such as roads, short grass and pine-needles in woodland. They should be used only in the short term and only if necessary.

Boots and bandages can protect the horse against injury. Well-fitting leather boots with foam lining and buckles, or plastic boots, are preferable to bandages. Overreach boots which have a buckle fastening can rub the horse's fetlock. Some experienced trainers are against using any leg protection in competition, for fear of them slipping, rubbing or tightening.

A constant check on the horse's health is necessary throughout the training period. The experienced event rider must also be a knowledgeable horsemaster, familiar with the anatomy of the horse and alert to the first signs of trouble. Knowledge of the functions of the organs and circulation enables the trainer/rider to make decisions about conditioning of the horse. A trusted and experienced veterinary surgeon who is experienced in looking after competition horses should advise the trainer and rider throughout training.

5. Competing in One-Day and Three-Day Events

Even though a one-day is not as strenuous as a three-day event, it should be treated with the same care and concentration.

Tack and spares must be inspected carefully, as for safety reasons they must be in first-class condition. A useful item is a stirrup leather which can be worn around the horse's neck, serving both as a spare and as a neck-strap to secure the rider over drop fences, etc. Light riders must check their weight and acquire a weight-cloth and lead.

One dressage saddle is needed – if the rider is used to it – and one cross-country saddle. Both saddles must fit well, especially at the pommel, where there must be enough room between saddle and withers, even with the rider's weight in the saddle.

In spite of the advantage of its light weight, a racing saddle is not advisable unless a rider is well used to it. No changes in tack should be made shortly before a competition. Horses with flat rib cages should wear a well-fitting light breastplate to keep the saddle from moving backwards during the competition.

The bridle for the dressage test in one-day events has to be a plain snaffle and in three-day events the same, or a double bridle. A well-schooled horse should go as well in a snaffle as in a double bridle; since many event riders are not so familiar with the double a plain snaffle might be the wiser choice. If a rider decides on a double bridle the horse has to be made familiar with it a long time before the competition.

For all other phases of the competition a plain snaffle – if necessary with a ring martingale – is most suitable. Although in three-day events the type of bridle is optional, a stronger bit should only be resorted to in special cases.

Stabling and lodgings should be booked well in advance. If the competition is not too far away it is a good idea to visit the venue and to arrange everything on the spot. A quiet, roomy box close to the location of the event should be found. The rider, too, should look for lodgings where he can find some peace and quiet, so that he can rest before the event and be able to concentrate fully when needed.

An early arrival one or two days before the dressage is desirable, to give the horse a chance to acclimatise. This applies particularly to the arenas, so the horse should be shown around as much as the rules allow. Keep the horse calm and relaxed: it is absolutely wrong to pick a fight with him, as he will get upset and be an unwilling partner in the competition.

5 (1) The First Veterinary Inspection

A three-day event starts with the first veterinary inspection. The horses are inspected in their starting order by the ground jury and a veterinary official. It is not obligatory but is desirable for the rider to present his horse, who should be turned out immaculately. The rider should also be properly dressed, either in riding gear or in a suit (with long trousers) – not breeches with training shoes!

The horse is inspected in hand, at rest and in movement, on firm and level ground. He must be stripped, wearing a bridle only. First he is stood up in front of the jury. The rider is then told to walk on and he leads the horse first in walk, then in trot, on a straight line away from the judges, does a right hand U-turn, and returns towards the judges. The horse is trotted out on a long rein and is inspected from the front and from behind.

In this first inspection and the second one after Phase C the decision of the ground jury as to whether or not the horse is fit to compete is final. Objections are not allowed.

Although a decision to eliminate ('spin') a horse might seem harsh to the rider, it has been made by responsible people. Their main aim is to save a horse whose condition would deteriorate should it be allowed to continue.

The warming-up period for the dressage test needs a lot of 'feel' and calmness from the rider, which will be transferred to the horse. The fit horse will be full of himself, and the main task of the rider is to bring him into a relaxed frame of mind without using up too much of the energy which must be kept in reserve for the next day. Usually the warming up is done with relaxing exercises and much walking in the vicinity of the dressage arenas. Even a tense and highly sensitive horse has to be brought on to the aids. Harsh actions are as wrong as 'not touching' the horse by trying to ride without a safe contact of reins and legs.

In the dressage test the judges are looking for a free, forward-moving horse without any tension, showing clear transitions within a pace and accurately-ridden movements and figures. The horse should be straight and in balance on both reins, accepting a light contact. The nose should be in front of the vertical. The FEI test asks for very little collection: and therefore hardly any lowering of the quarters and related raising or arching of the neck. The test should prove that the horse is obedient and agile enough to cope with a difficult cross-country course. The rider is not allowed to carry a whip nor to use his voice. Good marks will nearly always be achieved by a rider who sits softly and deep, with the upper body upright, low, still hands, and invisible application of the aids.

The cross-country is the most important, most difficult, and most beautiful part of any event. It therefore requires the most thorough planning and investigation. The following refers to the cross-country of a three-day event, almost all of which can be applied to a one-day event.

Preparation starts at home, with the rider familiarising himself with the rules and regulations. He may find many things of which he was not aware before!

After arrival at the venue the rider reports to the secretary's office, learns all about the set-up, and has a look at the cross-country course plan. He can walk the course only after it has officially been opened. He should do this twice, either alone or with his trainer. He should also walk the steeplechase course. Roads and tracks can be inspected by car or bicycle. The more the rider is familiar with the route, the more he will be able to concentrate on his riding. He must take a good look at the fences, decide how to approach them, note the conditions for take-off and landing, etc. But he should memorise only the important facts. It is a mistake to burden the mind with too many 'problems'. On the other hand, it is also wrong to ride even the smallest fence too casually, without strong enough forward-driving aids, because the horse, especially when tired, might be inclined to refuse.

At open ditches and spread fences the speed must be increased early enough (perhaps with a whip aid). At drop fences and jumps into water the speed must be distinctly reduced, thus giving the rider a chance to get the horse more between hand and leg and the horse an opportunity to look at the fence, which will make it easier to jump.

Every jump across country is different. But in general the rider should sit forward from take-off until landing, the seat out of the saddle, with deep yielding hands maintaining a light contact. From this position the rider can immediately restore control after landing and be ready to ride on.

A rider who leans backwards over drop fences, or when climbing down a slope, is behind the movement. Such a seat is a thing of the past. Sometimes a rider uses this outdated technique to avoid being thrown forward when the horse pecks on landing. It is also wrong, because the horse can regain his balance more quickly if his back is free, and when his balancing rod – his neck – has freedom of movement. To remain in the saddle the rider should crouch, 'make himself small', lower his centre of gravity, get a firm grip, and bring his lower leg with deep heel and knee a little more forward so that he can brace himself against the stirrup.

The important factor is the rider's will to win and to master every situation.

Thorough knowledge of every metre of the going in all phases of the endurance test, together with a correct assessment of the energy reserves of the horse, will dictate at what speed to ride the various phases. Uphill and downhill gradients will also play a part in the time calculations.

If the cross-country phase is not preceded by a roads and tracks phase the horse should be warmed up a little as for a jumping competition, which includes jumping a few fences.

The various phases of the endurance test of a three-day event merit the following considerations:

5 (2) Phase A. Roads and Tracks

(220 metres per minute) The rider should be at the start ten to fifteen minutes before the starting time, to weigh in, check tack, set the watch, etc. The start for Phase A as well as for Phases B and D is a standing start. Exceeding the optimum time in this phase is penalised with one penalty point for each extra second. Such faults are unnecessary and should be avoided. This phase is ridden in trot and, where the going is good, at an easy canter (350 metres per minute). This saves time, and means that a bad stretch of road can be walked, which will be easier on the horse and a better preparation for the next phase, the steeplechase. Changing pace helps the horse more than a constant fast trot without taking variations of the track into consideration.

In Phase A it is important to pick a good route. At a normal trot a tarred road is easier for the horse than an uneven grass edge or a deep sand track by the road side.

As the finish of Phase A is the start of Phase B, it is advisable to arrive two or three minutes early. You will then have time to shorten your stirrups and take another look at the steeplechase course. Between the finish of Phase A and start of Phase B there is a small neutral zone where the rider can walk the horse around until he is called into the box at the start of Phase B.

The rider has to enter this box in time to be able to halt at the start – but not too early, especially with an excitable horse. The horse may be held by an assistant. If there is a false start, the rider will be called back by a steward with a red flag out on the course. The time is measured from the *first* start.

5 (3) **Phase B. Steeplechase**

The optimum speed in a novice class is 640 metres per minute, and in an open class 690 metres per minute. Whether the rider tries to reach the optimum speed depends on the condition of the course, the fitness of the horse, and the schedule he has planned for the competition.

In any case, the rider should pay attention to the following points:

Over the first 300 to 400 metres the rider gradually increases pace, allowing the horse to find his rhythm. The first fence should be jumped at a somewhat modified speed. The rider rides extremely short in forward seat, easing the weight on the horse's back. The horse canters, 'basculing' into the rider's deep hands without pulling. On the straight the rider moves towards the middle of the course in order to approach the next turn correctly, placing his weight to the inside and maintaining a strong contact on the outside rein. During the turn an increase in pace should prevent horse and rider from drifting out. The rider must aim to ride controlled turns.

To clear the fence the horse has to maintain speed and stand well back. Getting close to steeplechase fences loses energy and wastes valuable seconds. This fault usually occurs when a rider 'blocks' with his hands or moves them backwards.

It can be difficult to hold a horse on the steeplechase. Sometimes a multiple giving of the inside rein, with a soothing voice, can improve the situation. Sometimes it is easier to allow the horse to choose his own speed at the gallop. This is better than the horse fighting the rider's hand all the time.

The finish of Phase B is also the start of Phase C, and this starting time is valid, no matter what the schedule states. After going through the finish of Phase B the rider, now on Phase C, pulls the horse up quietly and gradually, either on a straight line or on a shallow turn. A few hundred metres after the start of Phase C there is usually a 'box' with a farrier who can be used if needed. This is where the assistant should wait with the spare set of shoes.

Riders who have no shoe problems should give their horses a short break on a long rein. They can also lead them for a while, lengthening the stirrups at the same time to cross-country length. Phase C is then ridden at trot and a steady canter.

After Phase C there is a compulsory halt of 10 minutes. During this time the second inspection takes place – a brief examination conducted by two extra members of the ground jury and a veterinary official. To avoid having to trot the horse up for the jury, the rider passes the finish of Phase C at trot on a long rein. During the compulsory halt the horse should not be allowed to get cold and stiff, but should be walked around with a blanket and loosened girth. He should be refreshed by spongeing his mouth, nostrils, chest and belly. He also can be allowed to drink about two litres of water – more is not advisable.

The rider can take some light refreshment, and should use the next few minutes to concentrate his mind on the ensuing Phase D, the most important part of the event. He will be grateful for any news about how the competition is going.

He then mounts in time to have the horse 'on the aids' before starting out on the cross-country.

5 (4) Phase D. The Cross-Country

In Phase D the optimum speed is usually 570 metres per minute. This time can only be achieved on good going with horses who are able to gallop.

Going too fast by over-riding a horse in an attempt to avoid time faults will result in jumping faults, or will cause injury to the horse's body and limbs. The rider bears a great responsibility towards his horse. If he feels the horse tiring, he should reduce speed and bring the horse more on to the aids.

If he feels – maybe after one or two refusals – that his horse is running out of energy, he should retire and not push the horse hard to get round. Respect for the living creature must remain the supreme law in eventing.

After the finish of Phase D the rider rides back to the weigh-in area.

5 (5) After the Cross-Country

The sweat should be scraped off the horse immediately. He should then be walked around (for about fifteen minutes) until his breathing has returned to normal. Depending on the weather, the horse should, if necessary be covered with a blanket. Bandages should be removed, and the saddle area, chest, belly and legs sponged down. Washing the entire horse may only be done in very warm weather.

The horse should be examined for any cuts or injuries. Small cuts which do not need stitching should be treated immediately with antiseptic. Major injuries must be treated by the veterinary surgeon.

If possible the horse should be walked rather than driven back to his box, as this normalises the body functions more quickly.

If the horse returns to the stable dry he can be fed and watered normally.

Then check the shoes and take care of the horse's legs. Even if they show no abnormalities, after a short cold hosing they should be given prophylactic treatment. Medicines have changed considerably over the years and today in Germany most people use Enelbin. All had and still have the same effect: cold treatment followed by warm treatment increases the blood circulation around the joints, tendons and ligaments and this has an anti-inflammatory effect.

In the evening the bandages should be removed, the legs hosed, and the horse walked out and allowed to graze. Afterwards the treatment should be repeated, and the legs bandaged again for the night.

The following morning the horse should be watered and groomed. A little exercise, such as a walk and a trot (on the lunge), will then help to remove any stiffness.

Before the jumping test the third inspection takes place. It is conducted by the same jury and under the same conditions as the first inspection. Again the rider himself should present the horse.

6. The Jumping Test

Basically the same guidelines apply as for a show jumping competition. In the warming-up period the horse should be made supple with relaxing exercises and by jumping some small fences and combinations from trot. Shortly before the start, two or three inviting spread fences will help to make the horse 'open up' when jumping.

The actual course should be jumped in a free forward manner without allowing the horse to get too fast and flat, thus knocking down fences and incurring penalties.

Having returned home after the event with – it is hoped – a sound horse, the rider can allow him an easy week with only light walk and trot work. A total lay-off after the event is a mistake. Training should then be in preparation for the next event.

The rider should have a critical think about the last competition. He should realize what went wrong and should also assess, independent of the official result, if the horse lived up to expectations and what this could mean for the future.

If after a competition the rider makes a rational assessment, it will certainly prove to be a profitable exercise both for him and his horse.

Index